FEARFULLY, WONDERFULLY MADE

STEVEN KNIPP

Fearfully, Wonderfully Made

"If two people love each other, there can be no happy end to it."

–Ernest Hemingway

For David

Authors Note

Fearfully, Wonderfully Made is often used in a spiritual context and is derived from a verse in the Bible, specifically from Psalm 139:14 (New International Version): "I praise you because I am fearfully and wonderfully made; your works are wonderful, I know that full well."

Fearfully, Wonderfully Made can also be understood as a poetic acknowledgment of human beings' complexity, intricacy, and beauty. It reflects an awe-inspiring recognition of the remarkable nature of human anatomy, physiology, and psychology. In this context, 'fearfully' implies a sense of reverence or respect for the sophistication of our design, while 'wonderfully' emphasizes the marvelous aspects of our existence. This magnificence is also present in our daily lives as we experience exuberant moments along with horrible ones. We are reminded that everything we go through is meant to evolve the whole of our species toward a more enlightened version of ourselves. This memoir is about just two individuals, among the billions of lives on the planet, who loved each other.

This book contains subject matter that may be difficult for some readers. Please read with care. The events and experiences described here are all true, although some creative license was used to construct a cohesive story. Some names and identifying details have been changed to protect individuals' privacy. Conversations are based on my distinct recollections but are not intended to be precise transcriptions. Instead, I've retold them to evoke the true feeling and meaning of what was said, with awareness that almost no story belongs to just one person.

Contents

Part One

1991—1997

1

A Journey Without You. December 1991

stared at Tom's body slouched in his recliner, my mind paralyzed by what I was seeing. My eyes darted around the living room, looking desperately to anchor myself to anything else. The mauve couch and loveseat we had so carefully picked out together. The rectangular glass coffee table, framed in black lacquered wood, that Tom had loved so much. The ceramic Art Deco wall clock, the one I had been wanting to buy for months. I could hear it ticking despite time having frozen. I looked back at what I frantically wanted to avoid—Tom's face, waxen and drained of color, staring blankly at nothing. His hand was dangling over the armrest, an empty pill bottle on the floor. A tremor crept up my spine as I noticed the envelopes taped to the chair. A sickening thud of realization hit me squarely in the chest. The suicide notes. That thing we had talked about for months had done nothing to prepare me for this moment because it wasn't supposed to happen like this. The horror of his expressionless gaze gripped my body as I stumbled away, grasping for a memory of him still alive.

I could hear Tom's voice when he first introduced the idea. We were in the kitchen putting away groceries when he had had to sit down to rest from the mild exertion.

"I need to tell you something I've been holding back for too long."

I stopped what I was doing and turned to look at him.

"The last hospital visit scared me. I felt trapped like a prisoner. I don't want to die hooked up to tubes in a cold, sterile hospital room, languishing day after day doped up on morphine, half out of it, until I die. I don't want to go like that."

I stood there for a minute, trying to process his words. Up until this last hospital stay, he had been optimistic about curing himself of AIDS, so his sudden switch of mindset threw me. But then again, it was clear his efforts were not working. He was always fatigued and barely had the energy to leave the house. After two rounds of pneumonia, he tired easily and coughed throughout the day and night. What had he been secretly planning? Seeing the conflict on my face, he reached over and took my hand before continuing.

"I've lost control of everything. It was something I took a lot of pride in, the ability to control my destiny. I had a plan. When we met, I was pinching pennies to save for a down payment on a house. We moved to Seattle together to make a new life, but now that's pretty much over. I know this will be hard for you to hear, but I've been planning to commit suicide when the time is right."

I felt punched in the head by his words, unable to comprehend what he was saying. He wanted to kill himself? My shoulders hunched up as I folded my arms around my chest.

"You want to commit suicide?" I asked quietly. A cocktail of sadness and fear surged through me as I tried to keep myself from collapsing.

3

"Not right now, no," he assured me. "I want to have a plan, though, to figure out the details of how best to do it. I'll relax if I have something figured out."

My brain could understand what he was saying, but my heart felt squeezed by an invisible vise grip.

"What kind of plan do you mean?" I managed.

"How and when I'm going to kill myself," he replied. Before I had a chance to react to that bombshell, he moved on to explaining. "It's more difficult than you think." Suddenly, he became animated, his eyes bright with focus. "Especially if you don't want to leave a mess, which rules out guns, wrist cutting, or jumping off a bridge. The options you're left with are carbon monoxide or drugs. I figure overdosing on pills is the best option …." And then he stopped talking, noticing my mouth had dropped open. The words 'guns,' 'carbon monoxide,' and 'leaving a mess' were bouncing around in my head. Were we actually having this conversation? He made it sound like he was talking about which ice cream flavor to choose. Had I been so distracted with school that I had no clue what he had been consumed with? "Sorry about that," he finally said. "I've been thinking about this for months, alone, so I got comfortable with the subject. I didn't mean to overwhelm you." He gave my hand a squeeze, then asked what I was thinking.

What was I thinking? For starters, how about *Why the hell have you been planning to leave me?* But that quickly became overshadowed by another terrifying thought—What if he does this without me knowing? I tucked away my feelings and forced myself to sound supportive.

4

"Well, let me see. You're right about our comfort levels with the topic—I'm not there yet." I paused as my lip trembled and I fought the urge to cry. Tom pulled me closer and stayed silent. I went on. "I don't want you to die in a hospital either, so you should have a plan and get whatever drugs you need." I sat back so I could look at him. "I'm also clear about this," I stressed, locking my eyes on his. "I want to be with you when you die. I don't want to be surprised by finding you dead one day."

I plopped down on the floor beside Tom's body, trying to reconcile how he could have done this to me. Fury began to boil in the pit of my stomach. He had seen how relieved I felt when he agreed that I could be with him when he took his life. We had a rock-solid plan. The pieces had all come together several months earlier after meeting with our friend George. We were all having coffee when he told us about a suicide party he had recently attended.

"Suicide party?" I had asked. I flinched at the sound of it. I had never heard of such a thing. How could anything be more ghoulish than a party for a suicide?

"Oh, it's the latest thing some guys with AIDS are doing," he had replied. "A friend of mine, Peter, had a fabulous vacation on the credit card he knew he'd never have to repay; then he planned an elaborate send-off party with his friends."

I looked over at Tom, who was transfixed. George went on describing the scene.

"When I showed up, the house was filled with people, music, plenty of alcohol, and lots of laughter. Peter was holding everyone's attention as he entertained them with the most scandalous stories of his life."

By now, I was imagining Tom swallowing pills as I watched. Would I be strong enough to stand by and let him kill himself? What would I do when he stopped breathing? Would I freak out and try to resuscitate him? It was one thing to imagine being brave, but it would be quite another to actually watch my love go through with it. I wanted to tell George to shut the hell up, but he kept going.

"The most touching part of the evening was when Peter suddenly became serious. He stood up and said how glad he was that we were all there. Then he told us about his biggest fear since being diagnosed: dying alone. Through stifled sobs, he said that wasn't going to happen now. It was all very moving."

I realized that Tom was already sold on the idea. Once we got into the car to go home, he was clearly planning it.

"I know my sister will be there, and probably my mom and dad."

I sat in the passenger seat wishing we could talk about anything else. At the same time, the logic of Tom's decision started to make sense to me. He didn't want to be alone—of course! This way he could surround himself with loved ones at home instead of dying alone in a hospital. It stopped seeming like such a selfish thing to do. While he spent the next few months stockpiling a lethal dose of pills, I did the best I could to prepare myself for this new plan of his.

What I wasn't prepared for was to wake up to find his dead body.

Remembering the envelopes, I pulled myself off the floor and grabbed the one with my name. I opened it quickly, desperate to hear his voice even if it was in writing. His familiar scrawl provoked a fresh round of grief as my tear-filled eyes took in his message.

> *I'm so scared! A journey without you will be so lonely! I choose to commit suicide without your knowledge and do hope you will not consider this a breach of our trust. My reason for doing things this way was to spare you any guilt you might feel for not stopping me, and also to prevent any questions from the authorities as to why you didn't stop me. I love you more than you could ever imagine. You have enhanced the quality of my life a million times and I do hope we will meet in the future so we can continue our beautiful relationship. Until then, grieve quickly and let life go on. Love, Tom.*

I let out a cry of anguish, his final words tearing me in two. My eyes refocused on his opening words—he was scared. Tom had no idea what to expect once he swallowed the pills, and he must have been terrified. The vision of him alone in his chair, waiting to die, pierced my heart. But as I kept scanning his note, the fire of betrayal rekindled inside me. He hoped I wouldn't think this a breach of trust? How could it be anything but that? He flat-out lied to me. We had an agreement and he broke his promise that I could be there with him at the end. The months of planning and talking and preparation were all for nothing. My hands shook with anger as I tossed the note on the floor and grabbed the second envelope, marked for the authorities.

To whom it may concern: I have decided to end my life because the suffering of my disease is unbearable to me. This decision is known to others but the final decision has been mine alone in a normal state of mind. I am a member of the Hemlock Society ....

I stopped mid-sentence. Amid the shock, I had forgotten all about Tom's membership at Hemlock, an organization that supports the right to die. I grabbed the phone and punched in the number to Tom's caseworker, who had told me to call if anything happened. When Randy answered, my voice cracked.

"He did it ... he's gone." We had talked about Tom so there was no need to say more. He knew exactly how to respond.

"I'll call the coroner," he said after expressing his condolences. "Are you still with him?"

"Yes," I managed, looking over at Tom's corpse. I stared at the lifeless body, my head spinning, unable to take in the surrealness of it.

"Are you okay?" Randy asked after a few moments of silence. I was expecting this question because he had told us there was a high risk that I might try to kill myself.

"I'm as okay as you might expect, but I'm not suicidal." I was determined to put his mind at ease because the last thing I wanted was for him to come racing over with a shrink in tow. "Seriously, I'm fine." I wasn't. To get away from the body, I hid in the safety of the kitchen to wait for the coroner. As the minutes ticked away, I replayed the day before.

The AIDS Memorial Quilt was in town and we decided to attend the event. The quilt stretched for hundreds of yards, thousands of unique three-by-six-foot panels dedicated to individuals who had died. Each panel displayed the collage of a life: photographs, writings, artworks, and fabrics of all kinds. It was impossible not to think about a good friend of Tom who had died just a few days earlier. As we strolled along the convention center pathways with hundreds of others, the vast room reverberated with silence. The sole exception was a woman's soft voice slowly reading names from the stage.

"Michael Adams," she read from the page in front of her, followed by a long pause where stillness rushed in. Then she called out the next name, "Stephanie Milton," followed by another long gap of silence. Her voice became the metronome of death, of lives lost too soon. We walked up and down the pathways, our own predicament coming into full view. We both had AIDS. Tom was already deathly ill—an emaciated shell of himself. My blood tests were dismal. All I could think about was my name on one of those quilts.

I fell back into a kitchen chair, my head dropping between my knees in anguish. How had this gone so horribly wrong? Had this been his plan all along? Or was it the AIDS Quilt that made him change his mind? How could I have missed that? My mind drifted back to the previous night. As soon as we got home, Tom pulled me into a hug. We were both so emotionally and physically drained that we clung to each other, letting the warmth of our bodies sooth our rattled nerves.

Tom whispered in my ear, "Do you want to take a bath with me?" It had been a long time since we had done that because he was ashamed of the condition of his body. We soaped one another and touched with tenderness. There were no words, just the warmth of his touch that brought back the intense feelings of love I had for him. I wanted this never to end. Afterward, we settled on the couch to watch "Married with Children," our nightly routine. I drifted to sleep in front of the TV. Tom woke me and walked me to the bedroom. I crawled under the covers, groggy with sleep. He perched on the edge of the bed and looked at me soulfully, then leaned over and kissed my forehead.

"You know how much I love you, don't you?" he asked. I smiled, nodded yes, and asked when he was coming to bed. "I'll be there soon; I just want to finish up a few things first," he replied. He continued to look at me, wordless. Something in the way he was watching—with clear eyes and a peaceful expression—gave me pause, a sense I disregarded. Tom turned off the light and closed the door.

I snapped myself out of the memory and pulled myself up from the kitchen chair. My body felt heavy and defeated. As I stood there and looked around our apartment, the chilling silence consumed me. Tom was gone and I would never see him again. Why hadn't I been more attentive as he told me how much he loved me? Why hadn't I told him I loved him back? I should have pulled him next to me in the bed and held him tight. A fresh wave of grief engulfed me, my body trembling as I replayed our last moments together. It was the last time he would touch me; the last time he would say he loved me.

As I watched the coroner place Tom's corpse into a black bag, zip it up and roll it out of the house on a gurney, my mind fixated on Tom's suicide note. *My reason for doing things this way was to spare you any guilt you might feel for not stopping me.* What wasn't in that sentence was the excruciating subtext. He wasn't trying to spare my guilt; he was afraid I would intervene. It had been one of the things we had spoken about, because once he fell asleep he would no longer be in control; he knew there was a possibility I would call 911. I had assured him I wouldn't, but he wasn't willing to take that chance. He chose not to trust me. And while that stung, I also knew he was right—I would have tried to save him. As the weight of this truth pinned me down, my body shook with heartache. Tom was everything to me; he was my first love and the man I trusted with my life. Now he was gone forever.

An agonizing pressure started building in me and barreled past my lips as I screamed out an incoherent, deep-seated misery that had now become clear and present. I dropped to the floor, sobbing inconsolably as the reality of my situation hit: I was only twenty-nine years old and it was just a matter of time before the body in the black bag would be mine.

2

Desolation Sets In. January 1992

Grief can make you do strange things—like scour the bottom of your shower door with a toothbrush. Here I was on my hands and knees trying to scrub away the agonizing tragedy of Tom's death and my own impending doom. AIDS had now been ravaging the gay community for more than a decade. The deadly disease collided with society's intolerance and outright hatred of gay people. Many of us weren't out, so getting AIDS was like getting a pink triangle tattooed on your forehead; you were gay and you were marked for death. Being sexually transmitted ramped up the animosity from the religious and homophobic, confirming for them that we were being punished by God for our sinful lifestyles. I paid little attention to that cruel bullshit but, like everyone else, I was terrified. It was a disease that came on suddenly from a stealthy contagion that crippled the immune system, causing horrific deaths ranging from brain parasites to deadly fungal infections in the lungs. And now that I had AIDS, I felt like a ticking time bomb.

Tom's symptoms started with exhaustion. I found him resting his head on his desk at our real estate office one day when we were still living in Houston, sleeping, which was totally uncharacteristic.

Tom was a driven guy; sleeping on the job was against his nature. When I suggested a doctor, he flatly refused.

"If this is AIDS, I don't want to know," he said emphatically.

I stared at him, not sure what to say. Every part of me wanted to drag him to the doctor, but it was hard to argue against his point since there was nothing to be done about it. Instead, we tried to convince ourselves it was something else, because at the time AIDS wasn't too prevalent in Houston, while it was ravaging gay communities in New York and San Francisco. We knew of only a few with the disease, and besides, it came from sex and we hadn't been promiscuous in the six years we'd been together. Even so, I had a nagging suspicion because I knew that Tom, who was eleven years older than me, had had his fair share of sex partners before we met.

"Have you ever been to San Francisco?" I asked nonchalantly one day. I was trying to be subtle about it, but he must have understood why I was asking.

"I did have sex with someone there once," he answered, "but he was healthy and strong, so I didn't think it was risky at the time. And what can we do anyway? I don't want to start using condoms, do you?"

"No," I replied too quickly, because I was thinking maybe we should be more careful. Then again, if he had it, I already did too, so why bother now? Over the next few months, we tried to chalk up his fatigue to stress from owning a busy real estate office, so we decided to move to Seattle in the hopes it would give us a fresh start. I had enrolled in a graphic design college and Tom was going to get back into electrical engineering, something he was good at. But on the drive across the country, I began to worry. Tom had lost 25 pounds in the previous four months and slept for hours at a time in the car as I drove. Despite the tightening knot in my stomach, I kept hoping the move would fix things.

It didn't. Nearly a year after landing in the Pacific Northwest, I was in my bedroom when I heard Tom violently coughing. There was a thud and then a call from him, "Steve, help." Racing to the living room, I found him on the floor and knelt down beside him. His breathing was ragged and his face pale as I helped him sit up.

"What's going on?" I asked. Tom had grown steadily weaker and had lost another 20 pounds since our move. He had been slowly developing a hacking cough, but falling was something new. He was coughing so hard he couldn't answer me.

"We're going to the emergency room," I declared, pulling him to his feet, grabbing our coats and walking him slowly to the car.

Tom's belt was drawn so tight that his pants were bunched around his shrinking waist as we walked into the waiting room. He was so terribly thin that people stared at us, but I didn't pay any attention; all I cared about was getting answers. The doctor listened to Tom's chest and immediately ordered X-rays. As we waited for the results, we sat silent, unable to talk about what we might learn. I put my hand on his knee and smiled, mouthing silently *I love you*. He returned a smile that faded quickly as the doctor came back into the room.

"Have you been tested for AIDS?" he asked.

There it was. That word we had tried to put out of our minds. Everything began to move as if we were drifting through molasses. Tom's voice croaked out the word "No," and I was too frozen to speak.

The doctor looked silently at his notes before continuing, "Your chest X-rays revealed a pneumonia commonly found in people who are immunocompromised, as we believe you to be." Tom's eyes began to tear up; then mine did too. We both knew what that meant. The doctor left so we could process the news. As soon as the door closed, I buried my face in Tom's chest and we both cried. And then, as if on cue, ear-piercing sirens started screaming from the hallway, signaling the arrival of an emergency vehicle that had nothing to do with us. But, to me, the sirens were an ominous sign from the Universe: it was the beginning of our end.

* * *

In the weeks following Tom's death, I wandered around the apartment sorting through the remnants that remained of him: his clothes, his notebooks, his food, and the piles of supplements he had hoped would ward off the inevitable. There was no way I could get rid of any of it. My longing for Tom was so intense that I would bury my face in his unwashed shirts to be reminded of him. The cruelty of the disease overwhelmed me. Tom's final months had been particularly horrific. Not long after the pneumonia cleared up, a purple bruise appeared on his index finger. We knew what this was because others with AIDS had similar purple spots. It was a rare form of aggressive skin cancer. His finger became swollen, feeling tight and stretched, and the doctors recommended localized radiation therapy. After a few treatments, the swelling diminished and the pain subsided. But within weeks, reddish-purple lesions of various sizes began to appear on his face, and they quickly swelled into raised patches of irregularly shaped nodules with dry, crusty edges. An especially large one began to deform the right side of his nose. Tom was devastated. He was a tall, olive-skinned, handsome Italian man with black hair and a thick mustache. His eyes were a penetrating blue, and when he gazed at someone they became totally enthralled. Quick to smile, he drew the attention of both men and women who were hypnotized by his sexual magnetism. I remembered watching him in Houston not long after we met getting all primped up in front of the mirror, seeing him make sure his mustache was neatly trimmed and his hair was just so. Before putting on a shirt, he'd drop to the floor and do 50 pushups, then return to the mirror to pose with his newly swollen pecs. Next, he would put on a short-sleeve pullover shirt and admire himself all over again. To say he was dreamy would be an understatement. He knew it, I knew it, everyone in his path was enchanted. But now, my Mr. Dreamy had horrible lesions on his face, and there was no denying his affliction.

"I feel like a leper," he told me one evening while we were out on a walk. "People either stare at me or look away." I tried to be encouraging, reminding him how much I loved him and that I didn't care what he looked like. In private, though, I was looking carefully over my own body for any signs of the same purple spots.

As the days and weeks plodded on, the enormity of my loss settled into me. The dreams Tom and I shared of buying a house, making friends, building new careers, and growing old together were gone. I vacillated between missing him terribly and feeling simmering anger at his betrayal. How could he have done that to me? Why did he put me through his incessant talk of suicide if he didn't want me there? It had been tough enough adjusting to the

prospect of saying goodbye under the circumstances he had promised, but it was even worse now. The grief and rage was so intense
that sometimes all I could do was scream into a pillow as I curled
up on the couch, trying to release the pent-up fury that choked me
from the inside. But at night my mind plunged into abject terror.
In the silence, with nothing to distract me, my imagination would
sweep through every possible scenario, and the ending was always
the same: I was going to die. Tom was dead just two years after the
fatigue had set in, so who knew how long I had to live? There were
no symptoms now, but what did that matter? I was deadly conta-
gious with a sexually transmitted disease that was killing off thousands, which no one knew how to treat or cure.

A tornado of emotions roiled in me as I stared at the ceiling
night after night. The specter of sickness and isolation and dying
alone ripped through my brain as I replayed the nightmare over and
over. What kind of horrible illness awaited me? How much suffering
would there be? Who was going to be there for me when I got sick?
At least Tom had me to be with, but now, I had no one. The weight
of suffocating fear bore down on me, my heart fluttering at full
speed. Maybe Tom had the right idea after all—I should just get it
over with like he did. And yet, just the idea of being gone rocked me
to the core. A spasm of grief would wrench my insides thinking
about it. I was too young to die! I still wanted to travel and see the
world. I wanted to pick up and play my trumpet again. To be the
best uncle ever to my nieces and nephews. I wanted to build a new
career, and more than ever, to get another chance at love. But that
thought would force my mind right back to bottomless despair:
Who would choose to be with someone who was as good as dead?

3

A New Start. March 1992

It was a surprisingly mild spring day. The air was crisp and fresh, carrying the familiar sounds of birdsong that filled my ears with a thrilling symphony. I was sitting on the balcony drinking coffee with my best friend, Gary, enjoying this mesmerizing moment. It was times like this when I could temporarily forget the tragic circumstances of everything that happened. It never took long, though, before I would weave the conversation back around to Tom's passing. Gary listened for a while before stopping me.

"You know I'm your dearest friend," he started, looking at me intently, "and being here for you during this rough time has been a wonderfully touching experience. But honestly, I'm getting tired of hearing this story over and over. I think it would be better for you to consider talking to someone else about this too." His words stung. He was the only person I knew in Seattle who had known Tom before he got sick. There was no one else to vent to. Did he expect me to just keep this bottled up? "I know how much it helps you to talk about what happened to Tom, but there is only so much I can offer to get you through this," he continued. "Have you ever considered talking to a spiritual counselor?" My body began to relax. I appreciated where he was going with this. There was a softer edge to his words, and I realized he was just trying to help me.

"I have," I said, "Do you know of anyone?"

"As a matter of fact, yes," he replied. "His name is Father David Jaeger." Father? I screamed to myself. He had to be kidding.

"A priest?" I shot back. "Why would I want to talk to a priest about this?" It was out of the question. Just hearing the word 'priest' made my blood boil. I had left the Catholic church when I was seventeen, disgusted by what priests said about gay people. It was the church that made me feel such shame as a teenager. There was no way I was talking to a priest about being gay or having AIDS or any of it.

"Hold on, hold on," he said, trying to calm my rising protest. "Let me finish. I first saw him a few weeks ago performing Mass and his sermon blew me away. He runs the Catholic AIDS Ministry, a new program started by the church. He has a speakers panel of people with AIDS who share their stories. He's unlike any priest I've ever known." I sat there trying to make sense of his words. How could the Catholic church have an AIDS ministry? I thought they hated gay people. I was struggling to digest all that when Gary added one final thing. "And here's the real kicker; rumor has it he's gay. And he's cute too," he said with a wink. He's *gay*? How was that possible? The notion of a gay priest was incomprehensible—everyone knew what the church said about homosexuality. And besides, weren't priests supposed to be celibate? How could he be gay and stay a priest? Was he a sexless gay priest? What was the point of that? "Seriously," Gary said, sensing my hesitation, "he's special. Go meet him."

A few days later, I sat nervously in Father Jaeger's waiting room. I was still uneasy about baring my soul to a priest, but he had sounded nice on the phone and I was willing to try anything to feel better. But really, a priest? What the hell was I doing here? AIDS was bad enough, but suicide was taboo, and I had no idea what he might say about that. I consoled myself with knowing he must be a good guy if Gary liked him. Just relax, I told myself as I exhaled out loud.

Moments later, he walked in, looking nothing like I had con- jured. No Roman collar and black pants, just khaki slacks and a button-down shirt. What grabbed me first were his rich brown eyes, piercing and kind. He was over six feet tall, with a slender build, gold wire-rimmed glasses, and thick brown hair. The difference in our physical attributes couldn't be more pronounced: I was five foot four, had a well-proportioned build, thinning red hair, and dark blue eyes. When he smiled, I noticed a gap in his front teeth. Gary was right; he was pretty cute.

"I'm Father Jaeger, it's nice to meet you," he said, shaking my hand, "But please call me David. I prefer to be informal."

I followed him into the office and took a seat next to his desk. There was no doubt this place belonged to a Catholic priest; it displayed a picture of the Pope, one of the bishop, and a few col- orful paintings of religious scenes. My past feelings of belonging to the church began to bring back the self-loathing and shame that I had put behind me. I was tempted to get up and leave when David sat down.

"So, what can I help you with?" he said, which for some reason made me abandon my compulsion to take off. Perhaps it was his sincerity, which seemed to ooze out of him.

"A friend told me about your AIDS ministry and I wanted to learn more about it."

David smiled and nodded. "The ministry is for people living with AIDS and their families. The bishop asked me to reach out to those living with the virus, as well as to educate people in the parishes. It's been incredibly humbling to work with these brave young men and women who are dealing with such an awful disease." Those words landed with such tenderness that my eyes began to sting with tears. His voice had such a caring quality and his expression was laced with the kindness of someone who had deep compassion and empathy for others. "You said on the phone that you recently lost a loved one," he said, turning the conversation back to me. "That must have been incredibly painful. Was he your partner?" Tears welled in my eyes from my still-raw emotions. He handed me a tissue. I decided it was safe to tell him everything.

"Yes, he was my first partner and we were together for almost eight years. Once he was diagnosed, things got rough for him. It was so much worse than I thought it was going to be, especially when he started talking about killing himself." I paused to read his face to see how he responded to that, but there was no judgment in his eyes—only compassion. Before I could stop myself, I was spilling it all, my words tripping over themselves in a rush to get it all out. "He wanted to have the pills stockpiled in advance and we invited his parents and my mom to come and we were all going to say goodbye, but he decided to do it alone and it was shocking to find him dead in the living room, and now I have AIDS too ...." I stopped the avalanche of words as the familiar pressure of grief took hold of me. David remained silent as I composed myself. His quiet presence embraced me in a warm blanket of understanding and acceptance, the likes of which I had never felt from anyone before.

"I don't know what to say," he eventually replied. "Losing someone you loved and cared for, to have them die so horribly. That had to be devastating for you." It was all I could do to keep myself from breaking down completely. I knew I had come to the right place.

"Finding his body was a brutal reminder that my life is in danger, so I want to get past the grieving and get on with what time I have left. I'm exhausted by the replaying of what happened and the loneliness and uncertainty of my future. A friend suggested I come talk to you about the speakers panel and learn how I might get involved."

I could see him nodding as I talked.

"You would be a great fit for the panel," he encouraged. "Your story is heartbreaking and people need to hear it." He went on, "The purpose of the panel is to tell the stories of those who are living with and dying from AIDS, but we go further than that. Since we can't get around the issue of homosexuality, we tackle that subject head on. I like to challenge people's misconceptions about gay people, and putting a face to a story makes us less threatening and mysterious."

I felt the knot in my stomach begin to loosen. His gentle words felt as though they were wrapping their arms around me. He was acknowledging my pain. The dreadful fear that had suffocated my spirit was starting to loosen its iron grip. With just a few thoughtful sentences, his magnetic presence was doing more for me than all the wailing and floundering I'd been doing for months. At the same time, I was also baffled. Did I hear him say *us* when he mentioned dispelling false impressions of gay people? Gary had mentioned rumors that David was gay, but I couldn't shake the dissonance I was feeling about a gay priest.

"There is another piece of the ministry that's the hardest part— sickness and dying," he continued. "I take communion to people in the hospital who are very ill and, sadly, I conduct many funerals for young people struck down in the prime of their lives." It was comforting to hear him talk so openly about illness and dying. It somehow gave me a feeling of normalcy that I hadn't experienced with most of my friends. Many people dance around those subjects and don't know what to say. I could feel a connection building between us. And then my thoughts leapt back to the 'us' thing. Was this guy for real? It was impossible to fathom how a priest could be gay, let alone provide a ministry for gay people. I wanted to get to the bottom of this, but decided to start out slowly.

"It surprises me that the Catholic church allows an AIDS ministry. Don't church teachings say homosexuality is a sin?"

David's eyebrows raised. "That's an astute observation to make. Are you Catholic?"

I wanted to say, *Hell no!*, but I also didn't want to lose this connection with him. "Yes, but not a practicing one," I said. "I converted to Catholicism when I was young, but haven't been to church in years."

"Few gay people go to Mass anymore, and I can't say that I blame them. Who wants to listen to a priest saying homosexuality is immoral? The church has a deplorable reputation for supporting gay people."

They sure do, I agreed to myself. Recalling the old priest in my hometown blather on about the sin of homosexuality and the spiritual gifts of having a spouse and kids made me feel horrible about myself, knowing that would never be me. But David was unlike any priest I had ever met. As he talked, I nodded absently, his words dissolving into musings I kept having about whether he was gay. I needed to say something before I burst. When a break came in the conversation, I went for it.

"My friend heard rumors that you're gay. Is that true?" He smiled widely as if he were just waiting for me to ask.

"Yes, I recently came out. Kinda late, I know, but better late than never, right?" He smiled at me as I nodded in agreement. "I went through a personal rough patch a year ago but came out of it realizing I was a gay man and I had to acknowledge that to myself and others. Part of what I do is tell parishioners I'm gay—that usually gets their attention," he grinned mischievously.

This was incredible! I thought I was wasting my time going in there to talk to a priest who couldn't possibly relate to my story, but instead my mind was being blown wide open. He was clearly a rebel, but more than that, he exuded such confidence and self-awareness that it was leaving me speechless.

The best I could produce in response to his revelation was, "Thanks for telling me. Glad to have you on our side." I wasn't sure what was more interesting, an AIDS ministry in the Catholic church or a gay priest. When the conversation rolled back around to joining the speakers panel, there was no question what I wanted to do. "How do I sign up?"

4

Ice Broken. 1992

I paced back and forth in my apartment waiting for David to pick me up for my first parish presentation. A week had gone by since our first meeting and I couldn't stop thinking about him. The prospect of dating a priest—as ridiculous as it sounded—was starting to permeate my thoughts. It wasn't just his kindness that drew me to him; there was now a sexual charge that I couldn't shake. When I climbed into the car, he was all smiles.

"Are you ready?" he asked, his eyes bright.

"I think so. I'm a bit nervous, but glad to be here." With *you*, I nearly said.

"You'll be fine. Don't forget that people know what the subject is about and are attending because they want to know more. Feel free to be bold and honest. These are good people and I'm sure they can handle it."

I hung on to those words as we stepped into the sanctuary twenty minutes later and walked down the aisle to the front of the church. At least fifty people had gathered, and my stomach nerves clenched. Seeing all those strangers made my well-prepared talking points vanish into thin air. What was I going to say again? Oh, right. Tom. Suicide. Grief. AIDS. No wonder I was anxious. I scanned the crowd looking for furrowed brows, but no one looked agitated or uneasy. David stood up in front of the gathering and, after welcoming those who were seated, introduced me.

"We have a special guest tonight. His name is Steve Knipp and he's going to share his experience of living with AIDS." A hushed silence fell over the audience, as if saying the word 'AIDS' had magical power. I stood from my front row seat and climbed the three steps to the podium, trying to reassure myself that this was still a good idea. I looked out over the audience, my eyes catching on the stained-glass windows lighting up the back wall that screamed loudly that this was a church, the same type of place that rejected me as a child. I used to be sitting in similar pews, listening to the priests talk about the sins of people like me.

"My partner just died from AIDS and I have it too. My reason for being here is to share what it's like to have this disease so you'll have some idea of how devastating it can be—both for those with the illness and for their loved ones—who often feel helpless." I dove into my background about coming out as gay in high school, moving to Houston from Michigan to escape the judgment of some of my old friends, meeting Tom, relocating to Seattle, and the symptoms that led to his diagnosis. "He was sick for two years until he decided to kill himself because the suffering was too much. I woke up one morning and found his body." I choked up on those last words and stopped to collect myself. Haunting images of Tom flickered through my mind—the chair with his arm dangling over the side, the empty pill bottle, his cold stare. The looks of compassion mixed with horror from the audience made me wonder if those gruesome images playing in my mind were being projected onto a screen behind me. These people, strangers until just a few minutes ago, were glued to my story. I could see their teary eyes and nodding heads. It was clear they were feeling my pain, which encouraged me to share more. And so I did. I told them about the experimental medications I was taking and their side effects, about my worries of being alone and getting sick—about not knowing how long I had to live.

When I closed the talk and retraced my steps back to the seat beside David, the room was silent until someone in the back began to clap, and then they all joined in. I glanced at David, who was smiling and applauding with everyone else. He silently mouthed *nice job*. I glowed as a rush of joy and relief swept over me. Such a warm reception from the audience was one thing, but David's approval sent me over the moon. He registered my delight and affectionately touched my arm, sending shivers through my body.

"So how did you feel about the talk?" David asked as we got into the car to leave.

"It was incredible," I exclaimed, fully charged and still buzzing from the electricity of his touch. "I thought I would be nervous but, once I started talking, I knew this was just what I needed to be doing."

He smiled and thanked me for sharing as he pulled up to my apartment. As we said our goodbyes, his glance lingered and his smile persisted until shyness made me look away. I said a quick goodbye and climbed out of the car—then kicked myself for doing it. Heading back to my apartment, I was swept back to Houston eight years earlier walking home from the convenience store when Tom first passed me on the sidewalk. He was impossible to miss. I had noticed him in the distance, his distinctive bushy mustache catching my attention. As he approached, his eyes pressed into mine, signaling his interest, but I was bashful and kept on walking past him. Deciding to be brave, I turned around to see if he was still looking at me. He was, and it gave me the nerve to approach him. That single moment of daring launched our eight-year relationship. I vowed to have that same kind of daring with David from now on.

We delivered six or seven more talks over the next few weeks and enjoyed each other's company so much that we began adding walks and drives to the mix. Between our visits, I felt lighter, grinning spontaneously whenever the thought of him came to mind, which was all the time. I stuck to my vow to be more forward in our conversation, even as I struggled with some arbitrary line of who should make the first move. I thought he should be the one since he was taking the most risk, but walking this tightrope was driving me nuts. I was about to burst—I couldn't hold this to myself a minute longer.

"Tom's not even cold in the grave and you're already on to someone else," Gary teased when I brought it up. I knew there was some truth to what he said, but I was unwilling to wait around; the clock was ticking. Besides, I knew Tom would be happy for me.

Gary was excited about the shift in conversation and was glad that some of my old spark was returning. And though he hadn't intended to play matchmaker when he suggested I talk with a priest, he was encouraging and supportive.

"He's obviously interested in you," Gary said, after listening to me gush on about how well we got along. "I think the two of you would make a good pair." I was beginning to think so too.

During one of our increasingly frequent hangouts, David asked if I wanted to see where he grew up. Minutes later, we pulled up to a blue single-story home in the Green Lake neighborhood.

"This is it," David exclaimed, pointing to the modest home of his youth. As I studied the wood-framed, fifties-style house, trying to picture him playing in the front yard as a kid, he told me about how his dad reacted to his interest in the priesthood.

"I was twelve years old when I first brought it up with him," David said, gazing at the house as he recalled the memory. "He was less than thrilled, to say the least. He was livid, telling me in his gruff voice that "no son of mine is getting wrapped up in that church nonsense." I was upset by his reaction and knew he wanted me to show more interest in working in the construction company he owned. Over the next few years, I tried my best to help him build houses but, hell, I could barely swing a hammer, and I hated it! He laughed at the memory, and it warmed my heart to have him sharing this with me.

"I gradually wore him down, though, and just before my fifteenth birthday, I moved into Saint Edward's Seminary. It was such a high for me to be there, and it was everything I hoped it would be. The robes and the incense and the Masses in Latin every day—I was in heaven."

His version of heaven sounded like burning in hell to me. What twelve-year-old boy asks to go into Seminary, especially knowing celibacy is part of the deal? For me at that age, puberty was in full swing and my gonads were begging for attention. My best friend at the time, Ryan, was going through the same thing, and we discovered ways to help each other out. We'd pretend to be sleeping and let our hands 'accidentally' brush up against each other. That was all it took to get us so aroused that our pants flew off and we went to town on one another. It was our first time having sex and we couldn't get enough of it.

I looked over at David, trying to decipher the puzzle that he was. It was nearly impossible to imagine the kind of life he had lived. How could we be so drawn to each other with so little in common? Was I so desperate to not die alone that I was ready to jump at the first guy who showed an interest? And how would it work with him being a priest, anyway—Could he really date anyone? Would we have to keep it a secret, and if the church found out, would he leave me? And yet, I couldn't shake this deep knowing in my gut that we were right for each other. Then there were his words from a few days ago—that he was hoping to find someone to share his life with. I couldn't help but wonder if he was talking about me. Was he waiting for me to break the ice? Maybe he was hesitant because I was a volunteer with his ministry. I thought back to Tom and my vow to be more daring with David. Gary had even given me his blessing. What was I waiting for? I needed to stop being chickenshit about it and bring up the one question that had plagued me from the start: Was he celibate? It was an awkward subject to raise, but if he was into me, sex was key. Once we were back at his apartment and settled on his couch with cups of coffee, I decided to go for it.

"So, the thing about celibacy, is that hard for you?" I held my breath as I waited for his response. It must have been pretty obvious why I wanted to know. David's eyes gazed out the window; I could tell he was searching for the right words.

"When I first entered the seminary, sex was the last thing on my mind," he started, "But I was young and didn't know what it meant to be intimate. As I grew older and years went by without the touch of someone special, it began to bother me. I felt trapped by my vows of celibacy and the expectations of everyone who knew me to be a priest. Following my sexual identity crisis a year or so ago, I realized that celibacy was an unhealthy way to live. It was then that I had a life-changing realization: that mandated celibacy has done more harm to the men and women of the church than anything else, and I refuse to take part in being sexually stifled and intimidated." I felt like I had been holding my breath under water and had finally come up for air. It gave me the jolt I needed to press on.

"Have you had sex with anyone yet?" It was a bold question, but one I had to ask. I still wasn't sure if sex was just a conceptual idea for him or whether he was ready to actually do it. "A few times, yes, and I had no idea how much I was missing!" He grinned from ear to ear like a kid who had just discovered chocolate. By now I was ready to be whatever kind of chocolate he was craving. The energy charge in the room was tangible. My face heated up like I was facing the sun. He must have noticed because he got a quirky smile on his face.

"What?" I asked, smiling back playfully.

"Oh, nothing," he smirked, then fortified his look and said, "I was just thinking you look really good in that shirt … but I bet you'd look even better with it off." I wanted to rip off my shirt but decided to let him finish. "I know that's kind of corny, but I've been trying to figure out how to tell you I want to be with you." That

32

was all I needed to hear. I scooted closer, leaned over, and kissed him on the mouth. I had been imagining this moment for weeks and our lips locked together with a shared urgency. Once we were undressed and in his bed, I was overwhelmed by how good it felt to be naked and held by him. It was effortless to get wrapped up in his tall frame and be caressed with tenderness, gently erasing the months of loneliness that had swallowed me. There was a warm, earthy aroma that permeated the air close to him, like a walk through the forest on a sunny day. We both knew how to prevent exposure, so we brought each other pleasure carefully and lovingly. Afterwards, we regarded each other with fresh eyes, reflecting the sheer joy of what might lie ahead for us. I felt a deep satisfaction that went beyond words. My mind was clear, uncluttered. No more wondering about whether or not it was going to happen. After several moments of quiet, he turned toward me and rocked my world.

"I'm not naïve about how serious your illness is, but I have this deep sense of certainty that you aren't going to die from it." He pulled me in tighter and meshed his eyes with mine, "But also know this: I will be there for you if anything happens." I lay there stunned, with a lump in my throat. Did he just tell me he would be with me to the end? We had only known each other for a few weeks, but it was as if we'd known each other forever. He had more to say. "I also know that being with a priest might leave you wondering if the church will force me to leave a relationship. I have given this a lot of thought and I want to assure you that, while the priesthood is an important part of my life, being in a loving relationship is way more essential to me. I want to have both the church and you, but if I must decide between the two, I will leave the church." I was astonished that he had answered the biggest doubt I had about getting involved with him. As I continued to absorb the full import of David's words, my thoughts flashed back to my conversation with Tom when he first told me about his suicide idea. He knew I was terrified of being alone—of getting sick and dying without him being there—and he was doing his best to console me.

"I don't know what to expect in the afterlife, or if there even is one," Tom had said, "but if I can influence things to happen, I promise to send you someone to love." Although I had always been spiritual and appreciated his words, they hadn't done anything to quash my underlying fear or panic. But now, lying in David's arms, I could not shake those words. Tom hadn't just found me someone to love; he managed to locate the most adorable, trustworthy, eligible gay guy in Seattle.

And if that wasn't a miracle, I didn't know what was.

5

Confession. 1992

We were winding down the day in David's living room when he shifted his body in my direction and fixed his eyes on mine.

"If we are going to be together," he said, "I need to tell you something I haven't told many people because I'm not proud of it." He punctuated every word as he forced them out of his mouth. It was clear from the pained look on his face that there was a lot of hurt entangled in them. He had been such a godsend to me that I couldn't fathom him doing anything shameful. But he clearly had something he needed to get off his chest, so I offered him an encouraging smile and nodded for him to go on. I watched him stiffen, steeling himself.

"I was the priest at a church camp fourteen years ago and gave massages to teenage boys. Two years ago, one of the boys I massaged came forward and accused me of sexual abuse." He stopped talking as though he wanted to ensure I was absorbing what he was telling me.

I wasn't. His words came at me like gibberish. Sexual abuse? This phrase ricocheted in me, trying to find a place where it made any sense. How could that be even remotely true? Though we had only been intimate for a week, we had immersed ourselves in so many deep conversations that I felt I really knew him. On top of that, we had been naked together every night and he was nothing but gentle. The idea of him being sexually abusive was unfathomable. He started up again, interrupting my thoughts.

"It all began innocently enough. Getting the kids calmed down for bedtime was always chaotic, so I offered back massages to get them settled." That all sounded pretty harmless. I was following his story, but something didn't add up.

"I don't understand," I finally said. "How can a back massage be sexual abuse?"

David took a deep breath before answering. "The boy, now in his twenties, said it made him feel uncomfortable because, as I massaged him, my hand brushed against his genitals. It aroused him and made him feel violated by someone he should have been able to trust." David's voice cracked, as though his throat had snagged on the brutal truth of his actions. The slightest twinge of discomfort went through me on hearing that he had touched the boy's genitals. What kind of game had David been playing? If this was fourteen years ago, David would have been thirty-six and he should have known better. At the same time, I could tell he was sincere about his regret. And really, what *was* the problem? What teenage boy didn't get a boner from just about anything? I could feel a protective fire spark in me as I processed his story.

"I still don't understand," I said. "How can brushing up against someone's genitals be sexual abuse?"

David answered slowly. "Because it's how he perceived it, and that's all that matters. And it *was* abusive. I see that now. He said the guilt of the encounter ate away at him for years and made him feel like he had done something wrong. He withdrew from his family and started failing in school because he was worried he might be gay. I had foolishly convinced myself that massaging boys wasn't sexual, but I was just trying to find intimacy without getting caught. I took advantage of my position and I was wrong."

The boy, now man, was blaming David for being gay, failing in school, and withdrawing from his family? How could such a brief incident have caused that much havoc? Making him gay was a ridiculous stretch. I knew more than most how hard it was to come out, but placing all the responsibility for his sexuality on David made little sense. I felt like I was missing something. It was killing me that David was hurting over this. I could hear the anguish in his voice, and his vulnerability drew me to him even more. All I wanted was to hug him and tell him he did nothing wrong, but his body was tense, and I knew he needed to get it all out.

"Because of what I did, he no longer wants to be a priest, something he had dreamed of," David continued. "He sued the church for pain and suffering and got a large financial settlement." This detail set the flames inside me roaring. Money. So *that* was it. My stomach clenched because it all made sense now. That guy just wanted a payoff. The bile stung my throat now that I knew the truth; I was disgusted that someone would hurt and embarrass David in this way. "The whole thing made the archbishop realize there might be a scandal one day," David went on, "so he had to handle my case with extra caution. I spent six months at an inpatient treatment facility before I could return to work. That's the real reason I'm not in a parish and instead lead the AIDS ministry." A lightbulb lit up inside me. So that's why he didn't live at the parish and had an apartment instead; I had never thought to ask. I could barely believe David was wrapped up in all this, but maybe this was part of what being with a priest was like. I wondered what other bombshells might be coming.

David headed to the kitchen to put on some tea while I lingered in the living room digesting everything he had said. Parts of our earlier conversations deluged my mind. He had told me about being fifteen in the seminary and being required to confess any sexual thoughts or urges, especially if he masturbated. When he did, David said, he reported them to his confessor right away and was instructed to say one hundred Hail Marys and not do it again. He was punished for masturbating? It was absurd. No wonder David had made a mistake at camp all those years ago; he was unprepared and naïve about his sexuality. I knew from David that the seminary had other crazy rules, like not being able to visit home; David's family had to come to him. He also had to wear a head-to-toe black cassock everywhere he went and was not allowed to form close friendships; he was told they led to unnatural temptations. It was obvious to me that the church was largely responsible; making these kinds of outrageous demands on young men was bound to backfire.

By the time David returned with a tray of tea and cookies, I was thinking about the last item he had divulged: that he had spent six months in a treatment center. It sounded extreme. I was buzzing with curiosity.

"What was your time at the inpatient facility like?" I asked once he had settled next to me on the sofa. He took a long draw on his tea, and I sensed he was once again formulating his words.

"The counseling sessions were extremely helpful, but the main reason I was there was to prove that I wasn't a danger to kids. The archbishop needed to know that I wasn't a pedophile or likely to reoffend." The word 'pedophile' slammed into me, conjuring up images of creepy older men having sex with young boys. I felt that I knew David well, but in reality I'd only known him for a few weeks. What had I walked into?

"How did they prove you weren't a pedophile?" I was afraid to ask the question for fear of revealing my worry, but I had to know.

"It was truly humiliating," he said. "I was taken into a room and told to change into a hospital gown. Once seated, I was handed two small rubber rings and told to put them around my penis. A sensor was attached to the rings; then pornography was displayed and they recorded what aroused me. It was so embarrassing that I wanted to get up and run out of the room saying to hell with the church. But I made myself sit through it because I knew it would prove me innocent of pedophilia, and it did." I could feel my relief as I exhaled. The torment on David's face spoke volumes about how difficult this was to share; his brow furrowed as he described in further detail the testing and what it meant. He kept talking, but the image of wires attached to his penis was tough to shake. I would have been terrified about getting aroused at the wrong time since erections can be quite unpredictable.

David continued, "I spent months in therapy and support groups with people I grew fond of. When I was cleared by the therapist to return to work, I began to have hope that I might not lose the priesthood. I was relieved when the archbishop appointed me to the AIDS ministry because I could still be a priest and focus on something meaningful.

"By far the most important thing I learned at the treatment center was that my actions were quite reprehensible," David went on. "I was trying to fill an aching desire for physical touch by going about it in the worst way possible, convincing myself that because there was no sexual engagement with the boys that I was somehow innocent. It was excruciating to realize the harm I had unwittingly caused." He paused for a moment to collect himself before going on. "After spending many sessions in therapy dissecting my inner desires, I realized something critically important: I could no longer deny my need for intimacy, no matter the cost. When I got home, I was determined to open myself to love, and then you showed up! It was both a tragic and a miraculous journey to find my way to you." Yes, I nodded back, smiling with gratitude that he trusted me enough to share this painful story.

This new revelation careened around in my head as I lay in bed that night. While David slept beside me, I stared at the ceiling, filled with questions. Who was that young guy who decided years later to come forward and report something so explosive? He could never have known what his words would ignite; it was as if he'd lit a match to a stick of dynamite, dropped it in the middle of David's life, and walked away. Given what David said about realizing how badly he had unknowingly hurt someone, perhaps it was good that this happened, but still. What else was his accuser capable of? True, he had been paid off, but how could David be sure that the money would keep him quiet? I wanted to wake him up to ask these questions, but the poor guy had just spilled his guts to me—best to leave him alone. It didn't really matter anyway. I was so enamored of this amazing man that I didn't give a shit what he had done in the past. It was easy to stand up for him. He was the answer to my prayers. He could do no wrong. Instead, my thoughts turned to David here and now. Seeing him as a flawed human being just like the rest of us gave me a new respect for him. He took responsibility for his actions, and I admired him for that. It was hard not to remain incredulous at what the church had put him through. But, on the other hand, if none of that had happened, he wouldn't have been reassigned to the AIDS ministry, and we would have never met. It was awful what he endured, but lucky for both of us in the end.

I had thought I was the broken one, beaten down by grief and loss. Now I understood that David was broken too. A rush of determination surged through me; I was going to protect him as fiercely as he had vowed to protect me. I leaned into him, wrapping my arms around his waist. He stirred and pulled me in closer. We held each other tight, clinging to each other like life rafts.

"I love you so much," I whispered into his ear. "I'm sorry you had to go through such a horrible ordeal, but now you've got me."

6

A Life in Hiding. Fall 1992

"What do you think about living together?" I sprang the question on David as we sat on the patio eating breakfast. I had been staying at his house every night for months now, and it felt like a natural next step. As a practical matter, my lease was ending. David shifted in his chair, and I immediately sensed that he was uncomfortable with the subject. My stomach flipped over; this wasn't what I expected.

"Don't get me wrong," he finally said. "I love the idea of moving in together, but I need the appearance that we live in different places; otherwise, it might draw too many questions." His words were a huge letdown. I understood his caution, but felt disappointed, nonetheless.

"Okay, I understand," I said quietly, and forced a smile. He sensed my despair.

"It's not what I want either," he replied quickly, trying to cushion the blow, "but we need to be careful, at least for a while. Can we let some time pass to see if anyone notices?"

"Yes, that makes sense," I replied, trying to cover up feeling cheated that the church was getting in the way of our happiness. I wanted to ask him how long we needed to wait but knew that sounded desperate and pushy. I also wanted to ask how long we would need to keep up the charade, but I already knew the answer: as long as he was a priest, it was going to be like this.

I like to think that Tom, looking down from above, noticed my dejection, because within a few weeks he orchestrated another heavenly intervention: the condo next door to David's became available for lease. It was the perfect solution—deniability and convenience in one—so I snapped it up and moved in. Being next door relieved the living situation and made it super-convenient, but another problem appeared weeks later as we were heading for dinner.

"Father Dave!" a woman yelled as she came toward us on the sidewalk. She was so fixated on him that she didn't see me at first. "I thought that was you! How are you?" I noticed David stiffen up and that made me nervous; his eyes were firmly on her and avoiding me. This was the first time a random church person had seen us together in our neighborhood, and I felt a wall go up between us. I could tell David needed to pretend I was someone else and I wasn't sure I could handle it. On top of that, I was scared I would say something that might get him into trouble. The woman continued to talk about her kids and her husband and uninteresting churchy things. David listened and responded cordially as though I weren't there. Then I felt her eyes on me. "Who is your friend?" she asked, in a tone that in my paranoid state sounded accusatory.

"Oh, sorry, this is Steve," David said, feigning forgetfulness. "He's a good friend of mine. We were just getting some dinner." He quickly tried to change the subject, but the woman continued to look at me, not taking the bait. I bit the inside of my lip, trying my best to keep my face from giving away a guilty expression.

The woman ignored David, "Hi Steve. I've known David for years. How did you two meet?" Her eyes were piercing me so intently I was afraid she could read my mind. I felt exposed, as if I were on some kind of trial. I had no clue what to say. I looked at David, hoping he would intervene, but he said nothing. He just waited for me to answer. It was like being a bird pushed out of the nest for the first time; I was going to fly—or die trying.

"He was the priest at a Mass I went to recently," I lied, knowing I had to stay away from the AIDS ministry connection to avoid that whole subject, but it was a wrong move.

"Oh, what parish do you belong to?" Shit, I felt myself flapping my wings desperately. My head reeled as I tried to think of a parish I could name without getting more questions than I could answer.

"I don't belong to a parish right now. I was at St. James and he was filling in for the regular priest there." My heart was racing, praying that she didn't belong to that church. She nodded her head and returned her attention to David, who looked at me with relief as the woman prattled on about other things. I felt myself finally exhaling, grateful to have navigated the minefield intact. Once the woman was out of earshot, David relaxed.

"You did a good job staying vague in your answers," he said in a voice that told me I had passed the test. But just the mention of it riled me up all over again. We were seated in the restaurant and I had been trying to forget the incident. I knew David was attempting to make me feel better, but my nerves were on edge as he started talking about the encounter. "I should have warned you about that kind of thing happening," he continued. "We'll want to have a signal that says the person is safe to speak openly with or not, but if we get caught off guard like that again, it's best to say as little as possible." It all sounded so contrived. Having to worry about code words or whom to look for and knowing the right thing to say did little to relieve my anxiety. My stomach was in knots.

"But how will I know who is safe and who isn't?" I blurted. I could hear the frustration in my voice. I didn't want to be uncooperative, but this felt so unnatural and I was never good at making things up under pressure.

David listened, then reached under the table to take my hand. "This must be hard for you," he acknowledged. "I'm so used to keeping secrets that it feels like second nature to me," he smiled sheepishly. I could tell he felt bad and that made me feel worse.

"Don't worry about me; I'll get the hang of it," I managed, swallowing my feelings. "I just don't want to get you into trouble by saying the wrong thing. We need a system so I know when to stay and when to go, or what to say and what not to say." I smiled, trying to make light of my plea. David's face relaxed. Now that we were talking freely, a release valve had opened and all the pressure that must have been building in David came pouring out.

"I'm not entirely sure what to expect from my priest and nun friends," he said. "Some of them will be fine because they have partners of their own stowed away, but others might be less enthralled with the whole idea." His words were confusing me— they had partners stowed away? Maybe this was more common than I realized. "Don't worry, though; I know how to talk to them. I've known most of them for decades.

"I told one of my priest friends about you the other day and he wasn't exactly thrilled with the news," David continued, "but I suspect some jealousy." The words 'priest' and 'jealousy' collided; why would a priest be jealous of me? Was this friend in love with David? "We've been friends for decades and that's how we managed celibacy—platonic, lifelong companionship, but I knew he wanted more. He even propositioned me for sex a couple of times after I came out, telling me he just wanted to see whether he was gay or not."

Inside, I rolled my eyes, imagining a horny priest in church garb sidling up to David in the pew. I wasn't sure whether I should be jealous or feel sorry for the guy. "Really? That must have been awkward."

David nodded. "It was for a minute or two, but I understood what he was going through. You get affection and attention where and how you can. I know that only too well." Then, while I was still trying to digest this bit of news, he pivoted the conversation to his friend Susan, a nun he thought was in love with him. He told me his suspicions were confirmed by her chilly reaction to his disclosure about me. The idea that he had both priests and nuns coming at him was almost more than I could stomach. The ruse of celibacy was a farce, and besides, he was apparently telling his friends about me. How could I be expected to keep this secret when David certainly wasn't? And, as it turned out, it wasn't just priests and nuns I had to worry about; it was the gay community too. Some of the men we encountered were a bit too interested in finding out if David was available. There was a small gaggle of men who were members of Dignity, an organization for gay Catholics, and admirers of David, the handsome gay priest who danced around the issue of whether or not he was having sex. When asked directly, he'd get serious and say that he respects the laws of celibacy and follows them. If it was someone he trusted, though, he would add with a smirk, "but my confessor and I see each other a lot."

When we would run into some of these guys at events or on the street, they would look me up and down to see if they could figure out how close we were. The nosiest were those who had a crush on him and wanted to unseat me. David admitted he liked keeping people in the dark about it. It wasn't like that for me, though; sometimes I wanted to pull him into a deep kiss just for the shock factor.

My thoughts drifted back to my days with Tom and how carefree our lives were, at least at first. We had no one watching us or questioning what we did. Going to gay bars and Pride parades with complete freedom felt like a luxury compared to this. It had not occurred to me that David's hiding would also become mine, and I could feel the weight of that now. But really, how could it be any other way? Based on David's comments, gay priests must be pretty common, and of course they had to be careful if they wanted to keep their jobs. I stuffed down my feelings and instead focused on David and his clear passion for the priesthood. He was electrified when he came home from presiding at a Mass, his personality lit up with exhilaration. This was who he was and I wasn't going to get in the way. Besides, I had signed up for this. He was taking a risk, and it was only fair that I accommodate him, even if it meant staying under the radar.

7

The Retreat. 1993

A lthough I had not yet had an AIDS-related sickness, having a terminal illness messed with my head. I knew I should be worried, but instead I put it out of my mind most days. It was easy to stay in denial as long as I was feeling okay, but denial didn't quell the deep-seated terror that loomed under the surface, an indescribable foreboding I could not speak about for fear of unleashing it. Death. It was impossible to fathom my life coming to an end, so I placed the angst under lock and key. That is, until it all came crashing back at the Catholic AIDS Ministry retreat that David and I produced. The idea was born out of our ongoing speaking engagements and realizing that Catholics were hungry for more. I became so busy doing the graphic design and helping with the setup that it never occurred to me the retreat would be for me too.

It was Friday night and I was meandering around the meeting hall as 70 others were arriving for the first social event of the weekend. The energy was electric as people mingled. I felt proud of what we had created. The hall was a large rectangular space that served as both a dining hall and a meeting room. From ceiling to floor hung several paper banners painted with huge sunflowers meant to soften the cafeteria ambience, one of our many decorative touches. The rest of the place was utilitarian drab, and the guest rooms were sparsely furnished with a small bed, desk, and chair. We put flowers in all the rooms and gift boxes of stationery, pens, and chocolates to add a special touch.

Now that the planning was done and we were all there, I started to relax. The audience settled as David stood up and welcomed everyone with his opening remarks, looking around the room as if he were addressing each person individually.

"I called this weekend *Fearfully, Wonderfully Made* because of the theme of our gathering. We've come together under the crushing emotional burden of a devastating disease but, in joining our voices, we strengthen our resolve instead of being beaten by it." This was the first time I was hearing David's interpretation of the weekend's title. I looked around the room at the others, who were hanging on to his every word. "We have an astonishing capacity to love and endure anything life throws at us," David continued, looking directly at me. My throat tightened as I made the connection; he was speaking about our personal relationship. Something started to shift inside me. "We are here to experience our shared humanity by telling our stories of love and loss," he went on, his eyes connecting with others gathered. "To listen and learn from one another, and to come together in the spirit of healing." Tears welled in my eyes as I realized it wasn't long ago that I was lying in a crumpled ball on the bathroom floor, grieving like so many others here had done. How easy it had been for me to forget.

"It would be good to hear someone other than me talking," David said, smiling. "Would anyone like to be the first to share why you are here?" At first it was quiet, no one ready to plunge ahead. We were seated on folding chairs in a large semicircle, with people looking around to see who might start.

"I'll go," a voice finally sprang up from the silence. A woman named Sheila stood up and introduced herself. A hypnotizing hush came over the room as we all focused on what she was about to say. "My little brother has AIDS, and he hasn't told anyone in our family but me," she began, her voice shaking as she forced it out. She stopped for a moment to compose herself. "He tells me about the shame he feels and how hard it is to tell our parents. I wanted to tell them, but he made me promise I wouldn't." As she went on speaking, the dread of not knowing whether I was going to live or die came bubbling back to the surface. Nothing had changed; I was as vulnerable as ever. I had David, but I still had AIDS and, no matter what he thought, odds were I'd die from it. I took a deep breath and sat there struggling to stay focused on the words people were saying instead of on the pressure building inside me.

The next person to speak was a tall thin man with tattoos on his arms. "I'm here tonight because I'm lonely and afraid. I was just fired from my job at a hospital and I'm sick about why." He rolled up his sleeve and pointed to the HIV-positive tattoo inked into the crook of his arm. My eyes froze as I stared at it. "I got this tattoo when I was at the height of my addiction, injecting drugs into my vein right here," he said, pointing to it. "I wanted to be reminded every time I was tempted to shoot up that I was HIV positive because of my addiction. My employer felt very differently about it, saying it was making patients uneasy." My entire body began to tremble as I took in his words. Memories of Tom floated through my mind: his emaciated body, the coughing fits, the sores and deformities, and his cold, lifeless corpse. I shuddered, but kept a stoic face so others wouldn't see my mounting despair.

I held it together until the session was over, but I needed to get out of there before anyone saw me lose it. I pulled David aside. "I need to get some air," I said in a rush. "I'm going to take a walk." The minute I got outside, I let my tears fall. The cool breeze hit my face as I took in the lush surroundings of the grounds. Standing perched on a cliff overlooking the waters of Puget Sound, with the jagged edge of the Olympic Mountains in the distance, I felt like I was in paradise, and that made me cry even harder. The sheer beauty of the environs slapped up against the paralyzing dread I felt. I had found someone to love and wouldn't die alone, but now I just wanted to not die. To be swept away from all this beauty was more than I could bear. Deep down I knew I was living on borrowed time, and just because I had a priest for a boyfriend didn't mean everything would miraculously be okay. My heart began to race, and I had a sudden urge to run. I burst into a sprint, reeling from the avalanche of panic I had tried to tuck away. The need to escape felt primal, like I was running to save my life. I kept going until I was out of breath.

When David came into my room later that night, I lost it. "I'm not sure I can do this," I cried out. David took my arm and led me to sit on the edge of the bed.

"What's going on?" he asked softly.

"The stories people shared brought everything back. I couldn't stop thinking that I was no different from them; I could get sick and die just like everyone else." David just listened, letting me get it all out. "I've been pretending I'm okay, but there's still no cure, and you say I'm going to survive but everyone else is dying." I stopped to catch my breath. David wrapped his arms around me and I finally exhaled and relaxed into him.

"That's better," he said. We sat in silence for a few moments; then he spoke softly into my ear. "These are important emotions to have; it's good to let them out. Get as scared and angry as you need to feel. You can come to me anytime." I nodded and took another deep breath as he concluded, "I'm here for you no matter what."

The next morning after breakfast, everyone was given a choice of attending Mass or a yoga/meditation class out on the lawn. The meditation offering was my contribution to supply an alternative to the familiar Catholic ceremony. A sense of calm settled over me as I breathed in the crisp clean air, and exhaled the terrifying thoughts my mind had conjured the night before. Moving through the yoga poses and sitting in deep stillness was just what I needed to shake off the anxiety I had been experiencing. Afterwards, the afternoon sessions were posted. There were three break-out discussion topics: grief, relationships, and being gay in the Catholic church. Since I didn't care about being gay in the church, and my relationship situation was off limits, grief was the only remaining option. I groaned. I didn't need any more grief. Instead, I went back to my room determined to hold on to the calming effects of the morning. Drawing always relaxed me, so I grabbed my sketchbook and began flipping through it to find a blank page. The large inked letters of *Fearfully, Wonderfully Made* stopped me. I had drawn those words over and over to design the logo but, as I stared at them now, the power of the message David had spoken the previous night took on new meaning for me. How could life be so randomly terrifying and breathtakingly beautiful at the same time? A deadly virus was inside me, which struck terror deep in my bones. My life was indeed fearful—and I couldn't run away from it. But equally, it was brilliantly wonderful. Maybe my blood tests were a mess, but I felt fine. I had to remember that. It's what counted more than anything—if I could get out of bed in the morning, I was still in the game. And if I was still in the game, there was still hope.

That night, like the one before, David came to my room and stayed with me. I loved that he came back to console me, but when he slipped out again the next morning at 4:30 to avoid suspicion, I was reminded of the ruse we had been playing for over a year now. It was times like these that I grew weary of having to maintain a public façade. How long could I sustain living this way? As I headed over to the Sunday Mass that would close out the weekend, I overheard people speaking of another retreat. While we were glad it had gone so well, there was just no way I would sit through another weekend like this. After that rough experience the first night, I had shifted back into my organizer role and avoided talking about my personal life. Aside from the painfully raw emotions that retelling would stir up, pretending I had no one special in my life made it impossible to share openly.

As we drove home, David chattered on about the success of the weekend. I did my best to be encouraging, but I was reeling from what the retreat had unveiled for me. I felt like I was back at square one, the fear I had set aside resurfacing, ripping through me like it had never left. The death toll of my friends was mounting and I was sure to join them. David had rescued me from being

53

alone, but I couldn't have him out in the open. There would always be a reticent, looking-over-the-shoulder dynamic, and I didn't want that forever. I knew I would only have David for a little while, so I wanted to have all of him. My mind volleyed these agonies back and forth until my head was splitting. So immersed in inner turmoil, I barely noticed that we had pulled up in front of our building.

David parked the car and turned to look at me. His delighted expression took me by surprise because I felt just the opposite.

"I've been thinking about something I want to tell you," he said, reaching for my hand. "A friend told me once that there are three ingredients to happiness: *Something to do, someone to love, and something to hope for.*" He paused for a few seconds to let it sink in. "The only thing I was missing was something to hope for, but I've discovered what that is now: a robust and satisfying life with you. This weekend experience has reminded me how short life can be, and I don't want to waste another minute of it being afraid." His face lit up as if he knew that what he was about to say would soothe the pain he sensed in me.

"Despite my rejection of your invitation last year to move in together, I refuse to let the church have any more say about our happiness. Let's do it."

8

Experiment Gone Sideways. 1994

could sense David's eyes on me as I bounced around the apartment. "I think you should go see Dr. Meredith," he finally said, pestering me again to pay a visit to my primary care doctor. Why did I need her now? Just a week earlier, I had been writhing in agony from the relentless itching of a full-body skin rash but, now that I had some energy, David was worried? It made no sense to me. The doctor had told me the experimental AIDS medication had caused the allergic reaction, but Prednisone cleared it up and I was much better now. My creativity was bursting at the seams and I would work late into the night on graphic design projects. I had never felt better—why couldn't he just be happy for me? "I spoke to her last night and she thinks it's a good idea for you to come in for a visit." Fine.

"You look good," the doctor said as she came through the door and sat down next to me. "I'm glad you're feeling so much better, but David is right to be concerned." What? Now she's taking his side? I crossed my arms and tried to listen. "The Prednisone we gave you for the rash can have the kind of side effects you are experiencing—heightened creativity, sleeplessness, and your jubilant mood.

It may be triggering a manic episode and, if so, you want to get it under control before things get worse."

Great, someone else who just didn't get it. Why was everyone so worried? No one could understand what it was like to feel so miserable I wanted to die and, now that I am happy, there's a problem? I didn't get it, but I knew I had to cooperate or I would never get out of there.

"What do you suggest, Doctor?" I asked, doing everything I could to mask my growing ire.

"Lithium is the standard treatment, so I'd like to get you started on that today," she replied, as she pulled out her prescription pad and started scribbling.

"What kind of side effects should I expect?" She answered with the usual suspects, nausea and diarrhea, but when she said it may also cause drowsiness, I protested. "I don't want to be dragging my ass around all day, so I hope that doesn't happen."

"Some rest would do you good," she said, "but it shouldn't be that bad after a couple of weeks on the medication." A couple of weeks? Was she insane? There was no way I was going to be moping around the house for that long.

"Okay, I'll give it a try," I replied. She handed me the prescription and I left the office.

David was waiting for me when I got home. "How did it go with the doctor?" He was trying to sound nonchalant, but I knew better. He wanted me back to a regular sleeping schedule, getting into bed at ten every night. It was something I had readily accepted when we first started spending nights together, but I was tired of it.

Late nights were my favorite time, when creativity sparked my imagination and set my thoughts on fire.

My mind shot back to what David had asked. "It was good. She gave me a medication she said will help." I was trying to sound cooperative and had already decided to try one pill that night and see how I felt in the morning. If I woke up tired, all bets were off. "I've already taken the first pill, so we'll see." David gave me a hug, glad that I had taken his suggestion.

What I noticed first on waking was that my mouth felt stuffed with cotton balls. When I swallowed, my dry throat choked on the sandy grittiness of no saliva. I trudged out of bed into the living room where David was reading the newspaper.

"How did you sleep?" he asked, too bright and cheery for my mood. I was in the kitchen pouring a cup of coffee, trying to keep myself steady. My head was full of rocks conspiring to topple me over. There wasn't a chance in hell I was taking another pill.

"Good," I grunted. He looked over and smiled as I sat down on the chair next to him. "I'm a little groggy this morning, but not too bad," I lied, knowing that the ruse I was about to start would require some maneuvering.

Without the lithium, my energy returned in a few days, and I was feeling even better than before. Instead of taking the pill, I'd flush it down the toilet in case anyone checked my pill bottle. Stupid drugs—I was better off without them. But it was essential that I hide my subterfuge, so I continued to get into bed with David at the appointed hour, sneaking out once he was sound asleep.

Over the next few weeks, I felt better and better. Tears of happiness would appear with little warning. I was overjoyed by the sheer delight of being released from that horrible rash and the fogginess of the lithium. It was a new lease on life and I was going to grab it with a gusto I had never felt before. Having gotten behind on graphic design obligations, I worked for hours in my bedroom studio to catch up. A fresh level of creativity fueled my pen as I sketched and drafted the designs that were firing in my brain, often staying up late into the night. My clients were thrilled with what I was creating, which I thrived on. All I cared about was the internal font of creativity exploding in me and my wanting to get it all down. Notebooks became filled with sketches, ideas for business ventures, and random notes of inspiration.

David, however, was getting suspicious and more concerned by the day. "Are you sure you're okay?" he asked one morning after I woke with him at six, fully refreshed and energized. "I'm really glad you're feeling so good, but you have to be careful not to wear yourself down." He always said that, repeatedly telling me to take it easy. I was getting sick of hearing it.

"I'm fine, really," I said, and I was. I was fairly sure this was the mania the doctor had mentioned, but I felt so good I didn't want it to stop. Full of brilliant ideas, I was confident in myself. My body was invigorated, and I felt an enthusiasm for life that I had never known. There was so much I wanted to accomplish, and my days were numbered, which made me drive myself harder. That glimpse of what could happen to my health, when that rash came on, made clear the importance of every moment. David would come to understand.

I thought I was being clever sneaking out after David was asleep, but eventually I got found out. David woke up when he heard me enter the house.

"Where did you go?" he asked. Crap. Busted.

"Couldn't sleep," I replied, avoiding his gaze, "so I went for a walk. I need to finish up a work project. I'll be back to bed soon." David continued standing there, waiting for me to say more. When I didn't, he got right to the point.

"Are you still taking the medication the doctor gave you?" Uh oh. This was going to be impossible to talk my way out of; I was never a good liar when confronted directly. I weighed my options, knowing that if I kept lying I'd get caught sooner or later.

"I just can't take them, I'm sorry. They make me feel horrible." I braced myself, not sure how he'd take it. He stayed standing at a distance, not coming over to comfort me, which is what I was hoping for. He was always sensitive when I wasn't feeling good, so I thought my plea would get some sympathy.

"You can't keep staying up all night," he said finally, with a level of frustration in his voice I hadn't heard before. "It's not good for you and it's worrying me." Our eyes locked, his face stern and serious. The last few weeks between us had been a roller coaster ride. He was trying to understand me, this new version of myself who was more expressive, passionate, and charming, but was also stubborn and belligerent when boundaries were set at home. "I can't sleep when I don't know where you are or when or if you'll come home. We've talked about this over and over and nothing changes. I can't take this anymore. Will you at least go speak to the doctor again?" His voice made clear this was not a request but an ultimatum.

Dr. Meredith was not pleased. I was seated in her office getting lectured about not taking the medication, and that if I didn't pull it together, something awful was going to happen. "I've seen this condition many times, and trust me, you don't want to go there." After pausing to let it sink in, she went on with a plan. "I think it's time to give David a break and get you stabilized. There's a clinic that specializes in manic treatment. Let's get you checked in so we can properly monitor your recovery." I felt pushed up against a wall, so I acquiesced to her recommendation. "Good. Think of this like a health retreat; take some time off to relax and get better."

A health retreat? What a lovely idea. I imagined a luxury setting with spacious rooms, comfy beds, and a spa with a hot tub. The doctor made the arrangements, and David helped me pack. Imagining long hours alone, I loaded books and sketch pads into my bag. When we arrived at the front entrance of the center, I immediately grew suspicious.

"This doesn't look like a very nice place," I bemoaned as we walked down the dark hallway toward the reception desk. The walls were painted institutional green and the aroma of a strong antiseptic lingered in my nostrils. David was doing his best to remain upbeat.

"It's just for a few days," he said reassuringly, "and I hear the staff is really kind. You'll be well cared for." We'll see, I thought. I was already wondering if I had been duped. This wasn't a specialized health retreat; it was a psych ward. When I was taken to my room, the fantasy of luxury came crashing down. The twin bed slumped in the corner, a single chair next to it. The only other furniture was a rickety wooden chest of drawers dinged from years of use. Luxury this was not. The nurse was talking to David in the hallway, their muted whispers signaling that they must be talking about me. I picked out fragments of words: descriptors of hyperactivity and little sleep rose from their murmur. As soon as David left, I tried to get friendly with the nurse, Alma, who was assigned to me for the day. She was a tall middle-aged woman with silver hair combed tightly back and secured under a barrette. Her crisp white coat was accented with a silver pendant hanging around her neck. All very tidy. I couldn't tell whether she was a friendly nurse or some version of Nurse Ratched, the authoritative character from *One Flew Over the Cuckoo's Nest*.

"Can you tell me where the hot tub is?" I asked as soon as I was settled in the room. I had my housecoat and slippers on and was eager to relax in hot water.

"I'll show it to you later," she replied. Was that a smirk on her face? "The first thing you need to do is attend a group session that is just about to start."

"Why do I need to do that now?"

"Because I told you to, that's why," she replied quickly, then scurried out into the hallway. Nurse Ratched it was.

I arrived at the room where several people were already gathered, eight others arranged in a circle. When I sat down, all eyes turned to me.

"Could you introduce yourself to the group?" said the man with a clipboard. "My name is Dr. Swenson, and we're ready to get started."

"I'm Steve, hello, everyone," I muttered and retreated back into myself.

"Can you tell the others what you hope for while staying here?" the doctor asked.

Hell, this one was easy. "To use the hot tub after we're done and get out of here as soon as possible," I blurted out. Snickers from a few others made my cheeks flush with embarrassment. Looking around the room and listening to the inane things people were sharing made me realize I didn't belong here. Who wants to hear about lost careers and broken relationships? What a downer. When the group broke, I found Alma and made another request about the hot tub. "Can you show me where it is?" She gave me an annoyed look and pointed to my room.

"The only hot water can be found in your bathroom shower; go luxuriate in there," she said dismissively, as she turned to walk away. This place sucked. Any place had to be better than here. I started to hatch my plan to leave.

"I can't stay here anymore," I unleashed on David the minute he picked up the phone. "The place is filthy, the staff are rude, people walk around here like zombies … and there is no hot tub here like I was promised."

He let me get it all out, then made himself clear. "I'm sorry it's not working out like you hoped, but I can't get any sleep with you here. Can you give it another day and decide in the morning?" I reluctantly agreed, but after a night of strange sounds coming from other people in rooms next to mine, my mind was made up. I was determined to get out of there and into a proper spa setting. The image of a luxury hotel began to form in my mind; the Four Seasons downtown would fill the bill. It took a few heated conversations with the front desk nurse, but after I learned they couldn't legally detain me, I walked out with my suitcase and headed to the hotel in a cab. As we wove through downtown Seattle, the buzz of the city pulsated through me. There were people everywhere going in and out of office buildings and stores with bright signs flashing the latest sales. I needed to be in the middle of it.

After checking in, I dropped my things and set out about downtown. The day was cool, in the mid-forties and overcast. Walking down the street, a mystical experience came over me. As I looked down at the sidewalk, small stones embedded in the concrete sparkled. I visualized the stones as planets and myself as a great soul striding high over the Universe. I was in love with everyone who crossed my path. I felt interwoven with each one of them, accessing their deepest thoughts in a flash of telepathy as our eyes met in passing. Their happiness, or sorrow, or boredom, or fear would become my own for an instant, causing my heart to expand with compassion for everyone. When I happened upon a homeless woman shivering on the corner and begging for money, it made me wince with pity. Looking at her tore at my soul. I had to do something. I stopped and observed the storefront where I was standing: Pendleton. Beautiful blankets hung in the window. Perfect! Just what she needed. Inside, the colors and textures of the blankets were captivating, thrilling me with elation as I fingered each one. The spun wool woven into blankets was testament to the wonders of mankind's ingenuity. This was the best gift of kindness to someone exposed to the cold—a warm blanket made by skilled hands. I walked out loaded down with bags full of them, trudging back to the woman first. She didn't seem as excited about the blanket as I thought she would, but it didn't matter. No sooner had I left her when others began to gather, and they all wanted a warm blanket. I stood tall, feeling humbled and powerful at the same time. People were being drawn to me by some spiritual magnetic force field. I was a tuning fork that brought together the ones who needed me.

When I got back to the hotel, empty bags in both hands, I was reeling from the amazing experience I had had with the blankets and all the people I had met. I needed to tell David.

"You won't believe what just happened," I said excitedly, the moment he picked up the phone. Before he could reply, I resumed talking. "I just met nearly twenty homeless people downtown and gave them all blankets. Everyone was so nice and profoundly grateful for them. It was the coolest thing I've ever done." As I carried on about every detail, I realized there was silence on the other end. "Are you still there?" I asked.

"Yes. Sorry, I'm having a tough time understanding everything. I thought you were staying at the clinic. Where are you?" When I told him I had moved to the Four Seasons, I could hear him sigh with resignation. "So let me get this straight. Are you saying you handed out blankets to homeless people today?" His question dripped with disapproval. Jeez, there he goes again, raining on my parade.

"Yes," I replied flatly. How could he not see the beauty of this?

"How much money did you spend on all that?" That stern voice again. I should have just kept it to myself. I replied that they were only three hundred dollars apiece and worth every penny. He was silent but I could tell he was pissed because he was breathing hard.

"I bought them with my own money," I blurted before he could chastise me. "There was a shivering woman begging for money, and it made me feel I had to do something about it." This kind of plea usually convinced David to lighten up; he was a bleeding-heart priest and wanted to help anyone who needed it, but today he wasn't having any of it.

"You can't be spending thousands of dollars on blankets for homeless people; it's ridiculous," his voice rose in volume. I had rarely heard him this annoyed, so a twinge of guilt bloomed inside me. I quickly rebounded.

"I'm sorry, okay? I was just trying to be helpful." I stopped talking and hoped I had said enough to appease him.

"It's all right, I understand," David said, backing down a little. "I know you think you're going through something really big and important, but it scares me that you're wandering around downtown and spending so much money."

David was still talking, but his words became background noise as my thoughts wandered back to the hot tub. It was dragging me towards it with such force—there was nothing to do but obey. I waited for a break in the conversation.

"Okay, I'll be more careful with the spending," I replied quickly. "Gotta go now. I love you. Call you later."

9

Ecstatic Nudity. 1994

Every muscle in my body was turning into a puddle of pudding as the deliciously warm water tenderized me from the outside in. Each fiber hanging from my bones melted into the buoyancy that now embraced me. I closed my eyes and envisioned my body dissolving back into nature, becoming one with infinity. This is what I had been waiting for. When I eventually opened my eyes and rejoined my surroundings, I looked around at the spa and took in the features. It was exceptionally well appointed, with plush lounge chairs and colorful art on the walls. The quiet background music and delightful fragrance filled my senses with a wonder I could not escape. I became interlaced with everything around me, including other human beings, that flowed in and out of my acute awareness: there was the hunky man in a robe reading the newspaper, two men and a woman in the adjoining soaking pool, and the seemingly-married couple now seated across from me in the hot tub. Looking around at the half-dressed men stirred up my sexual appetite, which had been in high gear for the past two days. Handsome men I had passed on the street earlier had nodded and smiled, and I was certain they all wanted me. There was an unspoken conversation going on whenever I looked into someone's eyes.

They clearly knew I was part of the special tribe of spiritualized humans. I felt a deep-seated connection, a kind of mystical knowing what the other was thinking. Several conversations replayed in my head as I soaked in the exquisite swaddling of the water, a particular one rising to the surface. A guy I met earlier had mentioned that most luxury spas had clothing-optional hours after a certain time of evening, usually ten, and this thought had stuck in my head. I looked over at the clock. It was 9:55—how perfectly synchronous! Yet another instance that demonstrated my growing certainty that I was a superbeing.

The moment it struck ten, I casually took off my bathing suit and placed it on the pool edge. No one said anything. That guy was right! I was the only one participating, but that was alright; it was optional. After a while, I got out of the tub, bathing suit in hand, and walked back to the locker room, fully satiated.

Still in complete bliss the next morning, I headed to the hotel restaurant, my stomach hankering for steak and eggs. As I walked across the lobby, the hotel manager appeared out of nowhere. "Mr. Knipp?"

"Yes," I replied.

He motioned me over to the side, and I followed him. "We received a complaint from someone in the pool area. Were you there last night?"

"Yes," I replied. "What was the complaint about?"

"Were you naked in the hot tub?" the manager asked, staring at me. I flashed him my biggest smile.

"Yes," I replied, "I was told there is a rule that after 10:00 p.m. it's clothing-optional."

"Told by whom?" the manager asked, his tone incredulous.

"Didn't get his name," I shrugged.

"Regardless of what you were told, that's not our policy," the manager made sure to emphasize. "Do you understand?"

"Yes, and it won't happen again." I figured I could get along without a hot tub now that I had been in it once. I reached out my hand to seal the deal, but his hand was not presented. He had a stern look on his face.

"Sir, you must pack and leave the hotel immediately. This kind of behavior violates our policies of conduct. Security will escort you back to your room to ensure you have all the help you need to get relocated." He waved to the waiting attendant, who walked me to my room. Clearly this so-called manager wasn't from the same celestial league as I was, but no matter. I'll be the better human here and leave gracefully. He might learn a thing or two.

Once settled into the new hotel, I headed back out into the magical air of Seattle's retail core. The streets were lined with stores full of designer shoes and clothing, books and electronics, soaps and stationery, expensive salons and movie theaters, car dealerships and nightclubs. I was mesmerized by the massive variety of things we humans desire to buy. The colors called out to me, clamoring with their brightness for my attention. Over the next week, I weaved in and out of every nook and cranny of downtown and purchased whatever captured my attention. Books and belts and shoes and pants and watches and blank journals and art supplies and sketch-books. The trunk of my car was full, and so was I. Too full. When I talked to David each day, he encouraged me to come home when

I was ready. And, as I tired of my unmoored existence, I missed him more and more.

Just one more thing would complete this wonderous adventure. I wanted to mark its end with something grand, and a Volkswagen Cabriolet convertible was just the ticket. They were all over downtown and I just had to have one. I checked out of the hotel and drove directly to the dealership. Stepping out of my car, my eyes immediately spotted the one I wanted. It was a shimmering, dark metallic blue vehicle with a crisp white canvas top.

"I'd like to test drive that car over there." I pointed out the one to the salesperson who descended upon me the minute I parked. He must have known I was coming because the car instantly appeared, and as I sat in the driver's seat, the smell of new car and leather seats overpowered my senses. Driving around town as if I were royalty, intoxicated by the certainty that I was a member of the spiritual superelite, people would notice me and nod their heads slightly, signaling their recognition of my secret status. By the time I got back to the dealership, my mind was made up.

"I'll take it," I said to the salesperson. "What will it take to drive it home?"

"Not that much, really," he replied brightly. "All we need to do is determine the trade-in value of your Honda, negotiate the sales price of the new car, and then you'll be out of here." That sounded easy enough, and it was. Once we sat down, the paperwork was completed in a matter of minutes. He was probably part of the classified network and his job was to make my life easy.

"Do you have a price in mind for your trade-in?" he asked. I had no idea what it was worth and didn't care. I was certain they would offer me the best price they could; bickering back and forth over money was beneath our kind. When he offered me $7,500, I quibbled not a bit. Negotiating the price of the new car took only a few moments; they showed me the price tag and I said, "Fine." I wrote a check and it was done.

On the drive home, my excitement grew as I imagined how surprised and delighted David would be to see me, and even more so when he saw what I was bringing home. When I buzzed the front door, I asked him to meet me out front. "I have a surprise," I told him.

I rushed into his arms the minute I saw him, powerful emotions erupting from how much I had missed him. His face glowed with warmth as we hugged each other tightly. "I'm glad you're home," he whispered into my ear. His words melted me into his embrace. As he pulled away to look at me, his eyes landed on the car.

"Is that the surprise?" I nodded enthusiastically in response, but my face withered as the next words came out of his mouth. "I'm shocked that you made such a purchase without talking to me first."

I could hear the frustration in his voice, and it knocked the wind out of me. Like a plane falling from the sky, my fantasy took a nosedive. I was already secretly wondering if this car purchase was a bit over the top, and now I knew it was. My once-jubilant mood cratered in on itself, the first crack in my picture-perfect exploits. He was right. We always made decisions like this together. What was I thinking? We grabbed my things and went inside, my head hung low in deflation. When we walked through the door, I followed David into the bedroom and put down my bags. He must have sensed my crestfallen mood because he turned to me with a smile and hugged me close. "I've missed you," he whispered in my ear. "We can talk about the car later, so don't feel bad." I nearly lost it, his kindness a balm I needed desperately. "You must be exhausted. The doctor told me to give you these to help you sleep." I took the offered pills without question, knowing it was time to let David take over. We sat up for a while talking as my body began to sink into the sofa. The last thing I remembered was David kissing me goodnight on the cheek before, suddenly, it was morning.

My head felt thick, throbbing, and my thoughts were mired in a dense fog that shattered my hope of navigating back to my weeks-long ecstatic state. The car problem made its way back, settling like a dead weight in my stomach. Everything looked different, less bright, less alive, throttled back. I set aside the disturbing nature of all this when David walked into the bedroom with coffee and a newspaper. He was already showered and dressed. When he asked me how I was feeling, I grunted, "Hung over and sedated. What did you give me last night?"

"Sorry you feel so bad. Dr. Meredith told me to give you a heavy dose of Ativan to knock you out and bring you back to your senses," he grinned, trying to make light of it. "You've been flying too high for too long, young man. It's time to get your feet back on the ground." He was right and I did feel absolutely horrible. The ecstatic high was completely extinguished, and my body felt like I had crashed at high speed into a concrete pillar. David reminded me that it was Mother's Day and his mom was expecting us. I groaned inside at the thought of spending the day with his family. I was in no condition to be seen; but when David insisted everything would be fine, I acquiesced. While I sat at his parents' table trying to focus on my food, waves of shame and guilt coursed through me as I replayed the last few weeks. Running up thousands of dollars on my credit cards for hotels and fine dining? Blowing more thousands of dollars on woolen blankets that likely ended up in a dumpster somewhere? Expelled from the Four Seasons for public nudity? And to top it off, I had that stupid car! By the time we arrived home that night, I was saturated with embarrassment. I waited until we crawled into bed to say something. "I'm so sorry for everything I put you through. I didn't mean for it to happen."

"Listen," David said as he took my hand, "I know this wasn't your fault. You didn't know what the drug was going to do to you. And besides, you were so happy after the rash cleared up, I was cheering for you." He smiled widely before getting serious. "Honestly, I'm just relieved you didn't get physically hurt—it could have been much worse. Try not to feel bad—before you know it, this will be a fun story to tell your friends." As we drifted off to sleep cuddled together, the last thing I remembered was how much love I felt for this man.

Every time I looked at the ridiculous car I had bought, my insides would turn to ice and sink me into the bowels of depression. It was bad enough that I sold my perfectly good Honda Accord, but blowing forty-five thousand dollars on a car I didn't even like was making this whole nightmare impossible to get over. And, to add insult to injury, the Honda was the car that Tom and I had purchased to drive from Houston to Seattle. David knew this was important to me and had already called the dealer, but he had been given the runaround and told there was nothing they could do. We decided to tackle it together by going in person.

"How can I help you?" the sales manager said when we arrived at his office. He knew who we were and exactly what we wanted because we had made an appointment. He was being phony as hell.

"We spoke on the phone yesterday, and I wanted to address this with you directly," David stated succinctly. "This is my partner who bought the Cabriolet a few days ago." I was standing next to him, feeling like a five year old. The manager nodded briefly at me.

"I already told you there is nothing we can do. The sales transaction has been completed—it was a fair deal."

"Fair?" David spit out. "You paid him 3,000 dollars less than his trade-in was worth and sold him a new car at full price. Does that strike you as fair?" The owner shrugged as if he still planned to do nothing. "Is this how you conduct yourself with someone who was clearly experiencing a mental crisis?"

"He was acting normal to me," the manager smugly retorted, looking as though he was bored with the whole thing. "I'm not a doctor." This infuriated David even more.

"If this is how you treat your customers, I'll make sure to use my connections with the Catholic Church to let everyone know. This is a matter of social justice, and I'm certain they will help me spread the word throughout Seattle about your atrocious behavior." The manager was suddenly paying attention, especially after David informed him that he was a priest. David happened to know that the dealership was owned by one of the largest Catholic families in town. I knew he was bluffing; he would never use his position with the church as a personal bludgeon. But the threat seemed to be working.

"I'm sure we can take care of this," the manager promptly conceded. "Given the circumstances, we can make an exception and take the car back." Relief poured into me and I became overcome with gratitude. I looked at David, hoping to convey my immense appreciation. After I had gone off the rails, he was getting me right back on track.

10

Siren Call. 1994

A chill of fear shot through me when I first noticed it in the mirror—a small purple spot on the side of my face. I rubbed my finger over the slightly raised surface. It looked like the same thing Tom had had. Irregular in shape, edges tattered, it was a deep purple that had the look of a bruise, but brighter, angrier. Alarms screeched in my head. Tom was dead within a year of getting the same spots. The room tilted as my balance wavered. I took hold of the counter to steady myself. My heart began to beat wildly, so I took a few deep breaths to slow my racing, terrifying thoughts. Not this, please, I begged silently. My manic meltdown was fairly recent, but I had gotten back on my feet, and David and I had resumed our happy life. Another traumatic experience so soon could destroy the tenuous calm we had reached. I was afraid I'd start sobbing the minute David walked through the door, but by the time he got home, I had calmed down enough to sound normal. I forced myself to let him settle before blurting out, "There's something I need to show you."

"Okay," he replied casually, clearly unaware of what I was going to say. He followed me into the bathroom where the light was better; I pointed at it but said nothing. He moved in to get a closer look, then reached up and touched it. "Do you think it's KS?" he said quietly, nearly a whisper. I shuddered at his words. David had seen the markings of Kaposi's sarcoma before, so he knew what it looked like.

"I'm not certain, but it could be," I managed, biting my tongue to keep me from screaming what I was really feeling. He continued to examine it, stretching the skin in different directions to get an alternate view. I was looking at his eyes, hoping to see another possibility occur to him, but nothing registered. He finally stopped and pulled me into his arms. His comforting gesture drove home the gravity of what this meant. I howled to myself as I began to envision where this new discovery might lead.

"I love you. We'll get through this," he whispered. I kept my face pressed into his chest as he kept talking to me. "Let's not jump to conclusions until we've seen the doctor, okay?" I pulled my head away from his chest and nodded silently. David continued to speak gently, "We're in this together, don't ever forget that."

The next morning, we were in Dr. Meredith's reception room waiting to be called. David sat next to me holding my hand, and I held out hope that perhaps this was nothing. I smiled at him, silently thanking my lucky stars to have him with me. On the walls around us, soothing shades of green paint served to balance the large canvases of exquisite abstract imagery: black line art with splashes of color, one of them depicting a man's head, his hands arranging stars in the sky. The artist was one of the doctor's deceased patients. Dr. Meredith was adored by hundreds of gay men in the city for her compassionate care. She was the author of an anthology of poems describing patients' personal experiences of lost dreams, of sickness, and of dying young. She was a keen observer and a trusted keeper of our stories.

Once we got into the exam room, it didn't take long for her to appear. She got right to business, positioning a handheld light close to my cheek.

"You were right to come in," she said as she examined it closely. "It does have the telltale signs of KS, but let's get a quick biopsy ordered and we'll make sure." I nodded, but my heart sank into my gut. Images of Tom's fight with KS suddenly deluged my mind. Multiple doctor appointments. Hours in the hospital. Waiting and hoping for improvement, but instead watching his skin and joints get fried and seeing the whack-a-mole lesions popping up in the strangest of places. On the end of Tom's nose, a swollen nodule deformed its shape and partially blocked his breathing. The radiation reduced the swelling but badly injured his sinuses.

The technician took a biopsy the next day and cut out the entire lesion so, over the next few days as I waited for results, it was easy to imagine that, if it were cancerous, maybe it had all been clipped out. David continued to be pragmatic about my chances and encouraged me to stay strong and try not to worry. The certainty of his love kept me sane.

We were back in Dr. Meredith's office a few days later. I was fidgety, nervous about what I was going to hear. "The tests came back positive for Kaposi's sarcoma," she said, right after closing the door to my exam room. "It's in the initial stages, so I'd try not to panic just yet. I have a great oncologist I can refer you to." As soon as I heard the words 'Kaposi's sarcoma,' her voice went mute and all I saw was her mouth moving. David took my hand and squeezed it. I teared up and looked at him. His face was somber, fearful, not what I was expecting. It was clear how dire my situation was.

We were nestled together on the sofa that night when David brought up the subject suffocating us. "We know this kind of cancer is slow growing, so let's not get too worried," he said. His words sounded a lot more optimistic than the fearful expression he had exhibited earlier.

"I'm not worried yet," I lied, sounding more positive than I felt. In reality, a cannonball of dread had now lodged in my gut. I was foolish to think I might survive this, even if David thought otherwise. When he put his arms around me and kissed the top of my head, I buried my face in his chest and held him tightly, hoping he wouldn't notice the anguish sweeping through me. I knew that full-blown AIDS had finally made an unmistakable descent into our lives, and there was nothing we could do to stop it.

* * *

"Have you noticed this spot before?" the oncologist asked, pressing his finger lightly to a spot on my upper back as I lay face down on the exam table. David, standing nearby, came over to take a look.

"Is it another one?" I asked, my stomach clenched tight in a wasted effort to block myself from the news. It was bad enough having one on my cheek; I wasn't prepared for more.

"It appears to be, yes," was his reply. I looked up at David to make sure he had heard, and his hand went to mine. His touch coursed through me as I braced myself for the rest of the news. "We could biopsy it, but I'm sure it's KS." I could no longer take comfort in an isolated lesion—this crap might be everywhere. David squeezed my hand tenderly with unspoken understanding. I sat up and started dressing; the doctor was recommending radiation therapy and talking about side effects, but I was barely listening, replaying in my head what Tom had done. He was distrustful of Western doctors, so had decided not to get treated at all. Having read about the dangers of radiation therapy, he didn't want anything to do with it at first, even though it was less toxic than chemo. He endured four months of the lesions becoming swollen and painful before finally acquiescing, and by then it was too late. I wasn't going to make that same mistake.

I had the procedure the following week. Much like an X-ray, it caused no physical discomfort. Within forty-eight hours, I noticed a lightening of the deep purple color, and after two additional treatments, both lesions were shrinking in size.

"See? I told you they were getting better," David noted one Saturday morning as we lounged in our pajamas. We were both elated that the cancer was responding quickly, and I was soon off and running, determined to put this behind me and get back to my life.

However, the cancer wasn't done with me yet.

It wasn't long before I noticed a cluster of lesions on my torso. More radiation followed. Same good response, but I was reluctant to be too positive this time—and a good thing too. A few weeks later, another spot appeared on my chest, then one on my right shoulder, and another on my scalp. This was worse than what Tom had gone through, and my insides turned cold as I envisioned his body bag. Despite my mounting fear, David tried to stay positive. "Remember the essentials for happiness: *Something to do, someone to love, and something to hope for*," he said, quoting a favorite saying.

"And guess what? You already have all of those." He was gifted at sharing poignant insights at just the right time—something I came to call 'priest mode.' He was right; I had all three. Graphic design gave me something to do, I had him to love, and I hoped for survival. Despite the cancer, I was still hoping to live long enough for a cure.

I enjoyed my design work immensely, and that helped me maintain normalcy. Ironically, though, one of my clients was the Seattle Treatment Education Project, a local nonprofit that published an AIDS treatment newsletter. This was pre-internet, so information was hard to come by. Designing their publication, it was impossible to ignore the cold medical facts about various AIDS treatments, foretelling things that could still go wrong for me. The experimental drugs were causing major side effects and doing nothing to stem the dying. Travelling to and from the clinic for radiation therapy while reading about the failure of the current medical treatments did little to ease my skyrocketing anxiety.

The radiation treatments were repeated on those spots five more times. By the completion of the final treatment, the lesions had receded significantly, much like the previous ones now faded to barely visible. I held on to this latest victory but, again, the reprieve didn't last long.

Talking with the oncologist, David and I were worried. While the spots had responded well to the radiation, my right eye had swollen painfully shut. The doctor had just completed his examination and, judging by the look on his face, the news wasn't good.

"It appears the KS may be obstructing the lymph glands around your eye, causing the swelling," he said matter-of-factly. His words, though not entirely surprising, smashed into me with such force that I saw stars. What I had dreaded was now happening; the radiation wasn't working. This development with my eye kept me up at night because I feared KS was spreading throughout my body. "The cancer is proliferating in a substantial way," the doctor continued, "and I think we should consider a more aggressive treatment." I felt my breath catch. He didn't need to say anything more; I knew what that meant. I took hold of David's hand and focused on him to steady my reeling thoughts. He squeezed it and smiled faintly.

"What do you recommend, Doctor?" I asked, fully knowing the answer.

"Chemotherapy is your best choice," he replied succinctly. "Radiation is only viable if the lesions are visible, but with this latest eye development, it appears things are going on beneath the skin. The only way to ensure we treat the cancer growing inside is to do chemotherapy." Tom's voice started playing in my head, recalling all the reasons he refused to undergo chemo—that it was poison, always made you sick, and often didn't work. It had been a poor choice on Tom's part. "We'll use two drugs, Vincristine and Bleomycin, over a course of six weekly infusions …." The doctor went on but, since I had already decided to undergo the treatment no matter the side effects, I didn't care about those specifics. I just wanted to get the treatment started as soon as possible.

I went home to rest after finishing my first two-hour intravenous drip of chemotherapy and waited to see how bad it would be. David had prearranged my recovery area with magazines, sketch pads, and the remote control within easy reach, plus towels, water bottles, saltine crackers, and buckets for vomit. He had taken the day off to be with me. We hadn't been home more than thirty minutes when the effects of the treatment started to turn my body inside out. I pulled the blanket up over my shoulders as it started, a feverish chill sweeping waves of queasiness through me. Then the shivering began. My insides shook as if ice had suddenly gripped my bones. Within minutes, I was shaking so hard my muscles started to cramp up, and I cried out in agony, pulling on the kinked muscles in an attempt to release them. David brought the thermometer and stuck it in my mouth as my teeth chattered against the glass. My fever had shot up to 103. My head ached. My vision blurred and images began dancing around, so all I could do was close my eyes and try to stay calm. I lay under a pile of blankets trying to stave off the shivers when my stomach seized, churning my abdomen into a giant knot. Ignoring the buckets, I crawled out of bed toward the bathroom. David took my arm to steady me, but before we could get to the toilet, my stomach heaved up its contents so forcefully that the mess splashed over the edge of the sink and coated the adjacent mirror. Another upchuck was on its way, so David quickly maneuvered me to the toilet as the remaining breakfast erupted out of me. I continued to heave violently with my hands on the tank to brace myself and David standing behind me to keep me from falling. After it was over, I crawled back into bed, sweaty and panting from the exertion. My gut churned with nausea, the taste of chemicals and vomit coating the inside of my mouth. The toxins roiling around in my bloodstream kept my body glued to the mattress, my head throbbing with a sharp pain at the temples. So this is what chemotherapy feels like. I fell in and out of sleep as David, my sentinel, stayed nearby to comfort me.

Over the next few days, I spent most of my time resting in bed, aching everywhere from the treatment. The doctor had told us that the first time is usually the worst, and I hung on to that hope as I imagined the five additional treatments scheduled over the next five weeks. I now understood why Tom was so reluctant to try chemotherapy. Maybe he had been right. How could this possibly be good for me? Did I want to cripple my body like this? After four days of lying in bed, I managed to pull myself into the shower. As the warm water rushed over me, the cascade gave my body the cleansing it needed. I put shampoo in my hair and massaged it into my scalp, starting to feel just a bit normal again. As I rinsed the shampoo, I saw clumps of hair in the drain. I froze, not expecting hair loss to happen so soon. The mirror revealed patches of skin where my hair used to be. I reached up and pulled on the remaining hair, only to have it release from my scalp in chunks. The full weight of having cancer finally sank in.

After the second treatment, the oncologist expressed surprise with the dramatic improvement. The lesions were shrinking and fading in color, and the swelling around my eye had begun to subside. David and I felt encouraged to learn that this rapid improvement could mean the cancer was in an early stage. By the fifth treatment, my improvement was so significant that the doctor said the next and final treatment was unnecessary. The lesions, including those first ones that were radiated, began to vanish, leaving only a faint yellowish glow.

By the time New Year's Eve rolled around, David and I had something to celebrate at last. It had been eight months since the first spot appeared and now they were barely visible. We sat in our favorite chairs in the living room, David pouring two glasses of champagne. He handed one to me and gave a toast.

"Here's to the end of your cancer," he proclaimed as we clinked our glasses together. We were both smiling, but within me emotions collided: joy for having escaped this threat but unease and vulnerability about what might still come. There was no reason for David to know how I was feeling; I didn't want to spoil this moment of refuge. Instead, I raised my glass and returned his toast, "Yes, here's to the end of it."

11

Disabled. 1995

Dr. Meredith could be devastatingly direct when she wanted to get someone's attention, and she was definitely doing that now. "I know how important your business is to you, but your test results are not good," she said, her eyes piercing me. "You should seriously consider going on Social Security disability if you want to stay alive." Her words flattened me. I knew I had been taking a chance, but the test results made it undeniable. "Your T-cells are in the single digits," she added, punctuating her point. "This makes you extremely vulnerable to becoming sick." She had mentioned this before, but never so forcefully. I knew survival was all that mattered, but what would I do without my business?

Work was an addiction that started at age twelve when I became the star paperboy in my neighborhood. I was so good at it that a customer had written a glowing review in the newspaper after I delivered the papers in the sleet and snow. I had never felt good enough around my dad, but quickly learned that if I worked hard enough, the accolades made up for it, and I began to crave them. That success fueled me to try harder. When I was sixteen, I got a job in the kitchen at McDonald's and, when I turned seventeen, I was promoted to an assistant manager. After moving to Houston when I was nineteen, I started working at Red Lobster and, before long, I was training for a manager position there too. My next move was to the Four Seasons Hotel, where I started as a room service waiter and soon became Assistant Manager of the three onsite lounges. When I met Tom, I threw myself into real estate sales and within a few years was earning six figures. Work was something that got under my skin; it had a magnetism I could not escape—and that I did not want to lose now.

"Will you at least consider it?" I heard the doctor say, snapping me out of my thoughts. I told her I'd think about it. After fighting my way through cancer the previous year, I had decided to throw myself full throttle into my graphic design business. David had expressed his concern, but I was determined. Pulling it off would mean the disease hadn't won yet. With no concise business plan and naïvely underestimating my monthly expenses, I plunged in. I moved the studio out of our spare bedroom into a nearby office so I could properly expand the business. The first few months were exciting—outfitting the space with technology and furniture, new design projects coming in, and working with contract staff when needed. However, it didn't take long to notice the genuine cost of having a studio. I no longer had the luxury of taking time off when I wasn't feeling well; I had to keep churning out the work to pay the bills. Doctor appointments and medication side effects required considerable time and attention that were tough to juggle with the demands of my fledgling business. The invoicing, bookkeeping, city permits, and tax filings piled up, and I struggled to keep on top of it. Eight months in, after venting about it to my friend Paul, he volunteered to help with the bookkeeping. He quickly put things together and was the first to point out what I had begun to realize but was unable to say aloud.

"The expenses are eating up all your profits. You have to work a lot harder than before, and you don't always feel well. How long do you plan to keep this up?" It was the same thing that David had been asking. I knew they were right because I was struggling as I clung to denial. Some days I was firing on all cylinders, body and mind cooperating. Other mornings I would wake up with my tongue dry and sticky and a dense curtain of fog making thoughts blurry and disjointed. I had been pushing back at the warnings from David and Paul, but Dr. Meredith's doom and gloom prognosis was the last straw. Giving up my career was a hard pill to swallow, but it wasn't worth dying over. Still, what would I do with myself? I felt like a quitter. On the other hand, maybe this was just what I needed. Instead of busting my butt, shouldn't I be enjoying whatever time I had left?

I waited until after dinner to bring it up with David. "It's time to close the studio and apply to Social Security for disability." Even though I was confident in my decision, it still hurt to say the words. David pulled me in for a hug, my body calming with the comfort of his reassurance. "It's the right thing to do," he whispered. "And I'm behind you all the way."

Within six months, the paperwork had been processed and I was on disability, making me officially retired at 33. It was great at first. I could sleep late and take naps in the afternoon. I became part of an informal club of gay guys on disability who congregated at the Broadway Market for coffee, took long lunches, and spent a lot of time doing pretty much nothing. Without the stress of work, my health began to improve. But this was not the me I knew. Being productive with my time had become so ingrained at an early age that doing nothing felt like wasting my life. My mind jumped back to a motto from the high school job at McDonald's: *If you got time to lean, you got time to clean.*

Within a few months, I was back to questioning my decision—in large part because of its permanency. I'd wake up in the middle of the night, gripped with regret, my thoughts spinning in a relentless circle: If I work, it could kill me, but not working is killing me too. After obsessing about this for several months, I realized it was time to do what I said I would do when I went on disability: squeeze out as much life as I could before it was too late. David was eager to travel, so we started with that. My having inherited money from Tom gave us a budget, and not knowing when another illness would emerge created an urgency to get started. If I was going to die, I might as well have some fun.

We started in Italy. David had visited there once before and was eager to show me his favorites: food, architecture, ancient ruins, and above all, Catholic churches—dozens upon dozens of them. It was my first trip to Europe and I was blown away by the beauty of it all. Our next trips took us to Prague, Amsterdam, and Paris. When we weren't bouncing around the globe, we were road tripping across our own country, visiting places like Yellowstone National Park and Portland, Oregon. One of the highlights was a charter boat trip through the San Juan Islands, with David at the helm! I was floored when he revealed he could skipper a yacht, having picked up the skill from his childhood family boating trips. Although the traveling was wonderful, my mental wellbeing would ultimately take a beating as I let myself slip back into doubt about how I was spending my days. Was I really using well the time I had left? David and I were walking around Seattle's Volunteer Park when I voiced the struggle I was having. He listened, then went into priest mode.

"Those three ingredients to happiness, remember? You're missing one—having something to do." He paused to let it sink in, then kept going. "You love expressing yourself artistically, so maybe keep your mind open to another creative avenue." His words were so simple, but they ignited a new hope. I began to think about other possibilities. Two weeks later, the answer materialized when I was having coffee with a mutual friend who was a clay artist.

"Your graphics business was fine, but in the end everything you create ends up forgotten," she said. I couldn't argue with that. "Come to my pottery studio and I'll show you around. Who knows? Maybe you'll like it."

As soon as I gave it a try, I was hooked. The pottery wheel gave me a different way to create; instead of designing images on a page to sell products or promote a business, I was shaping a lump of clay to bring something completely new into existence. I spent hours on end every day basking in this newfound craft, throwing my body and soul into learning everything about it. It felt good to have some balance back in my life.

Thanks to David, I had restored that magic third ingredient to happiness, something to do.

12

Life Reborn. 1996

could hardly register the words being delivered by Dr. Meredith. "There's been a significant breakthrough in the treatment for AIDS," she said in a rush of enthusiasm. "It's a combination of multiple drugs that act on different viral targets. They've been testing it on people for the past six months and the results are so undeniably life-saving that it's been fast tracked through FDA testing—which means you can get some."

I gripped the phone to my ear. Still not grasping what she was talking about, I asked her to say it again. After repeating it more slowly, she ended with, "I think this might be the magic bullet we've been waiting for." My world tipped on its axis. Was she really saying I might survive? There had been at least a dozen supposed cures over the years that had fizzled out, so I was right to be leery. At the same time, I knew I was going to go for it regardless of the risks. The cancer had been in remission for over a year, but it had left behind a paranoia because I knew it was just a matter of time before another deadly surprise emerged. So I plunged in, taking a handful of pills three times a day and waiting to see what might happen. After a few days, my body began to react to the silent invasion of foreign chemicals. My mouth tasted as if I'd been sucking on a penny, and food would stall in my stomach for hours, stewing like rotted cabbage. I also struggled with exhaustion and a constant ringing in my ears. When I reported these side effects to Dr. Meredith, she assured me they were normal and that there was nothing to worry about.

"The body will adjust," she'd say, "Just give it some time."

Despite my misery, everyone I knew was touting this new drug combination as a revolutionary treatment, so I stuck it out. After two weeks, just as the doctor had predicted, there was a distinct drop-off of the side effects.

My spirits were hopeful but guarded, as David and I waited in the doctor's office to get the results of my first blood test, three months after I had started the new regimen. Dr. Meredith's enthusiasm was uncontained as she came barreling through the door.

"Your T-cells are climbing and your viral load has dropped tenfold," she said, grinning widely at both of us. "It seems to be working." David and I sat there, stunned, words stuck in our throats. Could this be true? Would this be the treatment that saves my life? David was squeezing my hand and beaming as we listened to the doctor go on.

"The main thing now is to carefully monitor your blood tests to make sure your kidneys and liver stay healthy, and to keep your viral load as low as possible. Let's check in next month," she finished, giving both of us a warm hug. David and I got into the elevator, flabbergasted. When the doors closed, David grabbed hold of me and hugged me tightly. A euphoria swept over me. Neither of us said anything, shocked into silence. Later that night it was a different story; we couldn't stop talking about the implications. The excitement grew as we imagined a longer life together.

"I can just see us now," David said. "I'm ninety years old and you're a spry seventy-one, pushing me around in a wheelchair. What a sight we will be!" As unimaginable as it sounded, who knew? While I tiptoed around the hope that this treatment might work, it brought back memories of everyone who had died. The faces of dozens of friends no longer on the planet ticked through my mind like confetti falling from the sky. Several people from the retreat had since passed away, their smiles and stories still echoing through my thoughts. David had performed hundreds of funerals and composed obituaries that filled an album we started so we'd never forget. Could this be the cure we had all been hoping for? And if it was, how was it that I might make it when so many others had not? What if Tom hadn't killed himself—would he have survived? My guilt about this—that pure chance might be on my side when the cure had eluded others—was hard to take. I thought about my friends who were still alive but too far gone to reap the benefits. Being transformed from a certain goner to a potential survivor warped my emotions out of shape. I wanted to be optimistic, but I was apprehensive. David knew how to settle the angst in me.

"Not to get all churchy-sounding, but you know I believe in miracles and this might very well be one," he said. "I know this isn't over, but you can choose to believe that the treatments are going to work. Trust what your body is telling you. Listen to it. So far, it's saying things are changing for the better. Let's enjoy that."

13

Provincetown. 1997

Life was amazing. It had been six months since starting the new medications and my T-cells continued to climb—so much so that I started to believe I actually had a chance of not dying so soon after all. And if that were the case, our sex life needed a boost. Like most couples new to each other, sex was incredible at first. David was starved for love and I was hungry for affection. But there was a certain mechanical nature in the way David approached sex that made it feel juvenile. That made sense given his late-in-life sexual self-discovery, but I was getting bored and wanted an occasional more experienced lover. But the last thing I wanted was to give David the impression that I didn't love him anymore.

At the same time, I knew he was at least curious about others because of how he drooled over the go-go dancing guys he loved to watch. We talked about our past sexual experiences, and clearly David had lots of catching up to do. He would joke that he could have sex every day and still not make up for lost time. That got me thinking he might be ready for it, and now seemed like the right time to jump in. We were headed to Provincetown, a New England paradise for gay men. Nude beaches, dance clubs, and shopping—P-town had it all. Sipping wine one evening, I decided to bring it up. "What would you think about opening up our sex life while we're in Provincetown?"

I let the question hang as David absorbed it. He grinned and said, "Go on, I'm listening."

"I thought it would be a fun time to try it out. Both our tongues will be hanging out the minute we get there anyway, so we might as well test it out and see how it feels. What do you think?"

David never responded immediately to an important question, and he paused for a few seconds to collect his thoughts. "Sure, okay, but only on one condition: If either of us feels jealous or uncomfortable, we call it off and talk it through. I don't want anything to come between us."

"That works for me," I replied, cheering inwardly because he agreed with my plan. "I'm not sure I won't be jealous, though, when I see you walk off with some cute guy, so I like your one condition."

David replied with the gentle tone I had come to love. "You know sex has never been the central thing for me—it's about coming home to you every night, being a family, and enjoying this amazing life we've created together. That's what matters most to me."

* * *

The gyrating bodies of hundreds of half-dressed, sweaty men packed the dimly-lit dance floor as the beat of disco bounced off the walls. Neon lights pulsated overhead as we stood on the perimeter when I noticed David had become fixated on a cute guy dancing in the crowd. The look of sexual hunger was stamped on his face.

"Go talk to him," I said, giving his side a playful elbow.

"Really?"

"Sure, I'll be over by the bar." A few moments later, he had joined his new beau and they were touching and whispering to each other. Before long, David glanced my way to signal he was leaving, then walked off the dance floor and left the club. Wow, that was fast. A slight pang of jealousy hit me. What if David likes this guy more than me? What if I don't meet anyone? Was I making a mistake suggesting this whole thing? The uncomfortable ruminations came to an abrupt halt when I noticed a stud across the room staring at me. He smiled when he got my attention, keeping his eyes glued to mine. He raised his glass and nodded an invitation. I pushed my way through the sea of bodies. When I got next to him, he told me his name was Rick. We made small talk before he decided it was time to stick his tongue in my mouth. As I eagerly accepted his advances, we made out for a few minutes, testing the waters for mutual passion. Judging from the rise in both our jeans, we were a clear match.

Rick moved his lips from my mouth to my ear and whispered, "Got a place to go?" Indeed I did. David and I had already worked out how to let each other know if we were occupied in our room. A rubber band hanging off the doorknob meant no entry unless it was an emergency. When I arrived back at the hotel with Rick in tow, I was relieved to find no rubber band. Once the door was closed, we tore off our clothes and wrestled each other to the bed. I landed on top of him, kissing him with an unexpected urgency. Rick was slender with curly dark hair, a scruffy beard, and a mischievous smile. I continued to writhe on him, his body hot under mine. Before long, he had his legs wrapped around my waist, positioning himself for entry. A flash of guilt struck me that I hadn't disclosed my health status, but I was too worked up to have that conversation now. The next hour was filled with sex like I remembered before AIDS—full-on fucking without condoms. The sexual liberation was overpowering, especially in light of the cautious sex that David and I practiced. Once we were finished, I was smitten. As I walked Rick back to his hotel, we chatted about our vacation and where we were from, but mostly flirted and caressed each other, both of us hungry for connection.

"Can I see you again?" I asked.

"Only if we get to do what we just did all over again," he said with a smirk. That we could do. I practically skipped back to the hotel, feeling sexy and desirable, pushing back the guilt-ridden thought that I might have exposed him to the virus.

When I got back to the room, David was brushing his teeth and getting ready for bed. He looked up and smiled through his toothbrush. After jabbering about the men we had been with, we got into bed and turned off the light, David's arms wrapped around me as he drifted off to sleep. My thoughts went back to Rick, bringing the deception back to mind. A pang of guilt stabbed me. Did I infect him? Should I have disclosed? What if he wants to have sex again? I want to, but should I tell him first?

The next day I couldn't stop thinking about Rick. I told David I was going for a walk with the guy I had met last night and that I'd be back before dinner. The main street in Provincetown was much like the bar scene, throngs of half-dressed gay men wandering around the shops and restaurants. My libido was in full swing, sexual prowess on high alert. Being on testosterone injections as part of my treatment made things even more intense. I was amazed at how much attention my well-defined shoulders and biceps drew from the kinds of men who had never noticed me before. My small frame was the perfect shape to carry compact muscles, and my ego was elated at this recognition. Rick was coming out of his hotel room when I walked up.

"Hey there," he grinned, seeing me standing outside. "What are you doing?" He was in gym shorts and a white tank top, his lithe body calling me back to the night before."

"Looking for you," I replied. There was a flurry in my stomach when I recalled our sexual abandon, and I felt an uneasiness about whether I was going to broach the subject of HIV status. "Want to go for a walk?"

He didn't answer right away, his eyes lingering on parts of my body that told me he had something else in mind. "Maybe after you fuck me again," he finally said, grinning impishly. There was no way I could refuse, so I put aside the question of disclosing for another time and followed him back to his room.

We were draped over each other in bed after the deed was done, and Rick was telling me about his life in San Francisco, his job at the Federal Reserve bank, and the pill regimen he was on for HIV. He said it so casually I nearly missed it. "Wait a minute, you're positive?" I asked, sitting up and looking at him.

"Yeah, is that a problem?" he shot back.

"No, not at all." I smiled. "Me too. I'm so relieved to hear that; I felt dishonest for not disclosing my status before we had sex."

"Oh, screw that shit," Rick replied. "I'm sick and tired of being held responsible for disclosing, and I refuse to do it. If someone asks me, I answer honestly. If no one asks, it's consent as far as I'm concerned." I had never thought of it that way, and it was hard to argue with his logic. Placing the responsibility of disclosure evenly on both parties made sense to me. It also felt good to be absolved, but I knew I'd have to think about that some more once I was out from underneath our heated passion.

When I arrived back at the hotel for dinner an hour later, David greeted me with an open smile and a hug. As I basked in his embrace and in the comfort of the relationship I had with him, I felt completely alive. After going through so much, I finally had it all.

Part Two

2002—2014

14

Swept Up by a Hurricane. 2002

David was reading the front page of the newspaper when I noticed his face had drained of color. Before I could react, he pushed it in front of me, pointing at the top of the page. "Take a look at this," he said frantically. I glanced down at the headline and before I could take it in, he proclaimed, "My priesthood is over!"

What on earth was he talking about? He seemed a bit hysterical, which was not typical. Our life had fallen into a comfortable routine and we were enjoying how our days had become so mellow. Thankfully, the funerals had pretty much stopped, but David was still promoting education and awareness through the AIDS ministry and standing in for vacationing priests to perform Mass, something he loved to do. I was still immersed in my pottery studio, where I continued to make and sell my wares. Entertaining family and friends with special dinners every month was especially fulfilling for us.

My eyes went from his crestfallen face to the newspaper headline: *Catholic church allowed abuse by priest for years*. I began scanning the article to see what he was so upset about. It was a breaking news story from an investigation by the *Boston Globe* about a priest who sexually abused boys. I was perplexed as to why this was significant to David because his situation was so different from this one. David gave massages to a handful of boys for a week and then stopped after overhearing some kids talking about 'Father Dave's massages.' He was mortified at the risk he was taking and never did it again. The priest in the *Globe* article, by contrast, was accused of fondling and raping countless kids over the span of three decades. There was no way the two could be compared, but when I got to the part about how the church was paying off victims to keep them quiet, a rock landed in my gut: This was the same thing the church did with David's accuser. Seriously? Are we going to have to rip the lid off this thing all over again?

I was trying to contain my growing fury as David stood up and began to rant. "Don't you get what this means? I am so screwed," he said desperately, pacing back and forth. Before I could grasp what he was trying to say, he had already jumped to the next thing. "The local press will be set loose, they'll force the Archdiocese to provide all the records, and then it'll be a witch hunt. I know how the press works. They will pressure the Archdiocese to release the names of any accused priest. They'll ask me to go on record, and if I don't, that leaves them free to speculate." David knew what he was talking about when it came to the press—he had served as Archbishop Hunthausen's media liaison for many years. And he was no stranger to controversy; he had been thrown in prison years ago, along with the Archbishop and several other peace activists, for laying on train tracks to prevent the delivery of nuclear weapons. They were all acquitted, but he had become savvy about how newspapers handle disputes. He went on anxiously, "I'll have to talk about the details of the back rubs and the lawsuit and my adolescent sexuality; it'll be so humiliating." His outburst ceased and he put his head in his hands.

I stood and wrapped my arms around him, his sobbing body shaking hard against mine. I'd never seen him like this before and knew I had to do something. As I held him, I realized it was my turn to go into priest mode. What would David say to me? I took a deep breath and went for it.

"This is really hard to go through, I know, but you did everything right. You put yourself through rigorous therapy and came out a healthier person. That gives you tremendous credibility if your story ever comes out." David looked at me, his eyes shiny with tears. "It's going to be okay," I said, "and no matter what, I'm here for you."

Although not assigned to a specific parish, David celebrated Mass most weekends. He was doing what he loved, even with the restrictions placed on his ministry years before. His priesthood being in peril had been the furthest thing from our minds. But what seemed like ancient history was now staring us directly in the face. And the more David talked about it, the more I realized how serious the problem could be. He understood how the church operated when in crisis, and this was definitely a crisis.

A few weeks later, the call David had been dreading finally came from the Archbishop's office. He retreated to the bedroom to talk in private. I waited until the door was completely shut and then pressed my ear against it to listen. For a long minute there was silence, but then I heard David's despondent voice break in.

"Yes, okay ... yes, I understand. When will this happen?" His voice was so sad even I felt like I had been kicked in the stomach. I heard him hang up the phone and made a beeline to the couch. When he came out of the room, he looked dejected.

"What did they say?" I asked lightly, acting as though I didn't already know it was bad.

"They are releasing a list of names to the press this afternoon, and of course mine is on it. They said they were calling me as a courtesy." He spit out the last word with disdain. His voice was harsh and the severity of the situation was suddenly very real. "I know what they're doing," he added, "I'm being thrown under the bus. The church will step aside and let public opinion run its course. It won't be long before the press is calling for a comment." That last thing he said lit a fire in me. Goddamn church!

The phone rang later that afternoon as if on cue. A reporter from *The Seattle Times* was doing a story on local priests accused of sexual wrongdoing and asked if David would agree to an interview. He had already given this a great deal of thought—it was pretty much all he had spoken about since the Boston story hit the news. That and all the unanswerable questions he wanted answers to. *Will I get to remain a priest? How will this affect us? What about my family? What about the parishioners? What about Michael, who brought forward the accusation? What would he do, especially if someone else came forward?* David would panic whenever he thought back to that time 24 years ago because there were others he massaged who might speak out. Even with his worries, there was no question that he would meet with the reporter. He was knowledgeable enough to understand that not speaking to the press would make it appear he was hiding something. He agreed to be interviewed that evening.

Over the next few hours, he fell into himself, consumed by anticipating the meeting. The weight he was shouldering had been growing over the weeks, and I felt worried about his physical and mental health. I watched him pace around slowly in front of our house, deep in thought, hands clasped behind his back, which he did when sorting out something in his head. When he came back inside, he was much calmer.

"Are you ready?" I asked. I could tell by the satisfied look on his face that he must have worked out his approach with the reporter.

"Yes, I know what I'm going to say." He was smiling now, more relaxed. "I have nothing to hide. Like you said, I was thoroughly examined and came out with a clean bill of health. That gives me the strength to take the story public." He paused and took my hand. "That, and you," he added. There it was, that spark of David shining through. This was the guy I loved; the fearless one. I couldn't stand what the church was doing to him, but at least he was fighting back.

Three hours later, he returned from the interview. He smiled weakly when I asked him how it went. "It was better than I feared," he replied. "She was respectful and I answered her questions as openly and honestly as I could. You never know how the whole story will come together until it's published but, no matter what happens, it felt really good to get this secret off my chest."

The night before the article was to be published, his optimism began to fade. It would be hitting the Sunday morning edition, the one paper nearly everyone read in Seattle. There was tension in the air. He was anxious, staring off into the distance. When he started talking, his voice was resigned.

"No matter how well the article is written, none of that is going to save my family from being dragged through all of this. Everyone will know what I did. My family and friends will be put in the awkward position of not knowing what to say." Even though David had shared this with his family years ago, I understood why he would feel bad about it coming back around again. While his family was nothing but supportive, it wasn't something they could easily talk about with their friends. I stepped close and put my arm around him, trying to be supportive, but I knew there was nothing I could say that would fix this.

We were up at dawn. The large headline grabbed our attention: *Seattle priest faces removal: "I'm so clearly not a danger."* We sat in the living room reading the story silently, the air thick with tension. David was afraid he would be misinterpreted, and I was worried about his emotional state if the story skewered him.

In the article, David admitted to giving massages, something he didn't understand to be wrong at the time. He described being mortified and deeply upset, genuinely concerned for the young man in question. He explained the circumstances of what happened by describing getting the boys settled down to bed at night, which was always chaotic. He told how he offered to give massages to calm the kids down and a few of them agreed. He recounted massaging them on the back, shoulders, buttocks, and legs, but left out the part about his roaming hands brushing their genitals. The story also indicated the very real possibility that he would be ousted, but stated that David thought his removal was unwarranted because he was "so clearly not a danger. It would be heartbreaking for me," he was quoted as saying. "I love being a priest. I love the church. I love serving people."

After we finished reading the article, we both sat silently, absorbing it all and trying to imagine the implications. David looked at me, waiting for a comment. Sweeping through me was relief that the article didn't present him as a monster and surprise that the reporter seemed to understand the complexity of the issue. It was also clear that David's personal life was now open for public scrutiny.

"I think she told your story with an empathetic undertone," I began. "She clearly was trying to understand. You explained your sexual inexperience at the time and took responsibility for it." David nodded his head as he took in my reaction. "You didn't justify your actions, instead explaining them in a way that should be obvious to many people. Most everyone knows that celibacy isn't healthy." David clung to my words as though they were a lifebuoy. I could tell he was feeling vulnerable, especially since he was scheduled to perform Mass in an hour. This had been his greatest fear since the initial accusation: public disclosure. And now he was going to find out what people would say.

David grabbed his jacket to leave. "I can't believe so many people will know all the sordid details of my sexual maldevelopment," he said as he headed to the door. "I have no idea what to expect when I get to church." I offered to go along, but we thought it better I stay home, which I was relieved to do. I gave him a hug for support, but as soon as he was gone, disturbing thoughts and emotions began to swirl.

We had talked a lot about how all this was affecting David, but we hadn't talked much about what it might mean for me. It dawned on me now that my friends would learn about the accusations against him. The 'ick factor' made it hard to defend, especially for those who didn't know David very well. Because of that, I had been extremely discreet in whom I had confided. But now there was no way of dodging the obvious question from others: Why hadn't I told them? Would my friends think I had been covering it up? How would I explain without sounding defensive that David was accused of only minor sexual indiscretion?

My blistering rage at the church was another thing. They caused this outrageous sexual catastrophe by mandating celibacy. Priests who were discovered became sacrificial offerings to siphon attention off the real problem, the church's unwillingness to relinquish the power of the celibacy mandate over priests. David's actions were minor compared to accusations against others, and I was angry that he was being treated like the worst of them. The church dragged him through hell—including extensive counseling and personal humiliation—and had done everything they asked of him. The idiotic notion that the church itself was not involved in the unfolding scandal made my face flush with anger.

I tried to imagine the intense scrutiny David was facing. I spent the morning pacing and wondering how it was going for him. Although I had braced myself for his return, David walked in all smiles.

"You won't believe what happened," he began, while hanging up his coat. "No one said anything before Mass, so I carried on as if everything were fine. Sitting on the altar chair looking out at the congregation, my mind ran wild considering all the horrible things people might be thinking about me." David stopped to take a drink of water, his eyes glistening with emotion. "I was picturing the hateful things they were thinking, like "Who does he think he is talking to us about God when he's the sick one?" It was even worse at communion as I placed the wafer on their tongues; there were averted eyes, expressions of bewilderment or pity written on the faces of quite a few. By the time Mass was over, I wanted to get out of there fast, so I exited through the back door."

"I thought you were excited to tell me what happened," I jumped in. "That doesn't sound so great."

David grinned; the lightness evident in his face. "That's when things changed. A middle-aged man approached me, someone I've seen many times but never spoken to. He introduced himself and asked if he could talk to me about the newspaper article. I didn't know what to expect, but it turned out he wanted to thank me for standing up, telling me it was courageous. It floored me." David was overcome momentarily with emotion, touched by recalling the man's kind words. When he recovered, he said brightly, "The good news is that if others have a similar reaction, I might get to stay a priest." I could feel his hope returning as he continued to speak. "This guy had strong opinions about celibacy and understood my predicament. He thought the church should be held accountable. It was amazing!" David's eyes remained moist as he stood there, relieved and delighted that this first public encounter was so positive. I could feel my own spirits lifting as David's excitement filled the room. Maybe he would weather this after all.

15

The Hurricane's Aftermath. 2003

In the weeks following the news story, David was embraced by many in the church. Much to my relief, my friends and family remained supportive; they knew him and viewed the whole affair the way we did. Letters of understanding and calls for forgiveness were being published in editorials; more were sent to the office of the Archdiocese, and many were sent directly to David. People were asking smart, thoughtful questions about sexuality among the clergy and most agreed that celibacy was to blame. Parishioners would stop him to say they prayed he would get to stay.

"How can the Vatican kick me out when I'm getting such positive feedback?" David asked after he read yet another supportive letter. "Maybe this will be okay." We both started to believe that his priesthood might survive.

Then we felt smashed by a sledgehammer. It started when we saw the name of the reporter he had spoken to last time flash up on Caller ID. David shot me a worried look as he picked up the phone. He listened for a long moment before replying that he would think about it and get back to her.

"Think about what? What did she say?" I asked, gleaning from the look on David's face that it wasn't good.

"She asked if I would do another interview, this time to respond to Michael, who has apparently come forward to tell his side of the story." His words knocked the air out of me.

"What? How can he do that? Didn't they pay him hush money?" I was livid. That guy was not only in it for the cash, but now he also had the spotlight he craved. Hadn't he caused enough damage? I was also pissed at him for being so duplicitous. David had told me that he and Michael had reconciled years ago, not long after he returned from therapy and started the AIDS ministry. Despite looking like he was going to cry, David quickly came to Michael's defense.

"I know why you're mad, but I understand how Michael must feel. The publicity around all this must be pretty upsetting to him, rekindling painful memories. He has the right to tell his side of the story too." There was that empathy again. It was one of David's best traits, but right then it felt completely unwarranted. I bit my lip and nodded my head.

The next day there was an even bigger blow. David answered a call from the Archbishop's office; he was being placed on administrative leave, effective immediately. His face was crestfallen as he relayed the details.

"They said I caused a media uproar, a scandal. Until this is resolved, I will no longer be able to function as a priest." His voice cracked and he paused, his eyes filling with tears. There was nothing more devastating to him than to not be a priest. This was bad. I found it weird that the call came before the story even came out; maybe they already knew what Michael had told the press. I took

David's hand as he went on, slightly more hopeful, "Maybe this will pass if I'm out of public view for a while."

That night, we were approaching sleep when David suddenly jumped out of bed and started pacing around the room. "What will I do for a living? How are we going to pay the bills? I'll never get a job at my age." The barrage of words spilled out, his voice laced with panic. Finding a job was something he never had to do before, and when it dawned on me that we both might be unemployed, his panic became mine too. We had savings to last for a while, but how long would this get drawn out? A chill ran up the back of my neck. What am I going to do? Could I even find a job now? Who the hell was going to hire me after being on disability for the last eight years? As hard as it was, I forced myself to switch to problem-solving mode so he wouldn't sense my growing worry.

"You have lots of skills to earn a living. You could start your own business, do weddings and funerals and spiritual counseling services," I offered enthusiastically. "You know people love what you do." The frown on David's face told me he wasn't buying it.

"I'm not an entrepreneur, and besides, not having access to the inside of churches limits my appeal for weddings and funerals. And counseling requires state licensing, which means more school. I've already thought about that. Just forget about it." I could feel the irritation in his tone. His admonishment stung, but I swallowed giving him further advice and told myself to stay out of it. But how could I? Our lives were so interwoven that, however this played out, both our worlds would be upended. David was the primary bread-winner, and I had no idea how we were going to make it.

A few days later, the article was published on the front page of *The Seattle Times* with a rather innocuous headline: *Zero tolerance, or forgiveness of sins.* Like before, David and I were side by side on the couch, each of us reading our own copy of the article, silently absorbed in the story. I scanned the first paragraph, which laid out the same details I had heard before. But as I turned the page and continued to read, my eyes landed on Michael's words. He thought what David did was "a shameful assault at the hands of a priest he idolized." My breath caught, but there was more. "There's an undertone to what Jaeger said, that 'What I did wasn't that bad.' What I'm saying is it *was* that bad." His words knocked me flat. I had convinced myself that David was the victim of celibacy, and that was the end of my thinking about it. But the jarring, emotionally-charged characterization by Michael made it clear that it wasn't the whole story. He stated he was confused and terrified when David started to rub his legs and buttocks, and when he slipped his hand under his leg bands, brushing against his genitals and touching his rectum, it terrified him even more. He touched his rectum? This part gripped my insides—David hadn't mentioned that detail before. Returning my focus to the article, David told the reporter he had been thinking at the time that "massages felt better direct than through material," and went on to say, "if I brushed up against his genitals, it was not deliberate, and I don't remember it." I had to stop reading to slow my breathing. How could he say something like that, and especially to a reporter? Did he really think that? This was way worse than David had led me to believe. My stomach was suddenly twisting up into knots. David had always told me that he purposely avoided doing anything that would be perceived as sexual, but there was no way this wasn't sexual. How was touching someone's rectum not deliberate? He made it sound like it was an accident, but that was impossible. Whether he remembered it or not was hardly the point—it all sounded so concocted that I could hardly stand to keep reading, but I needed to finish it.

Michael said he wanted David to both stop and go further, but he was aroused and ashamed—and convinced he would be in trouble if he said anything. To make matters worse, Michael explained that he was going through puberty at the time and grappling with the possibility that he was homosexual, which the church told him was a sin. He stated that he wondered at the time if Father David had been drawn to him because of that. Or, he fretted, was that the night that made him gay? Michael had been only thirteen years old when David molested him. Coming out was hard enough on its own. But to be tormented by thinking that the priest he worshipped might have played an insidious role in his sexual orientation must have been mentally and emotionally devastating. Michael was clearly a devout young Catholic—when I read that he had collected newspaper clippings of the Pope's ministry and statues of saints as a child while his friends collected baseball cards, I could imagine the chain of fear and confusion Michael must have endured while being assaulted by the handsome priest. It made me sick to think about it, and it was hard to wrap my head around the truth that it was David who did it.

My eyes went back to the story, which went on to describe the unimaginable suffering Michael experienced after returning home from camp that summer. His mother immediately noticed something was wrong. "His bubbly, open personality had changed," she said. "He was quiet and had a faraway look." When she eventually found out what had happened, she said "I felt so guilty. I felt like I delivered him there—to camp." My eyes welled up at this, thinking of my own mother. She and I had always been close, and I knew it would have devastated her if my personality suddenly changed with no explanation. I continued reading, now completely gripped by Michael's story. He had kept it a secret for ten years until being cracked open emotionally after attending a training session about the appropriate touching of minors that was, ironically, held at the same camp where David gave him the massage years earlier. During the training, everyone was asked to draw a picture of a time when it felt good to be touched by an adult. Michael drew one of his mother hugging him. Then he was asked to do the same thing when he was touched and felt uncomfortable. He froze. That's when he began to tear up and left the room. For the first time, I really got why he felt the need to come forward. For Michael, this wasn't about money or limelight, but about exposing the devastating toll taken on his life and about trying to stop this from happening to anyone else. Every assumption I had made about Michael's motivation was flipped on its head. I had been entirely wrong. And making that awful conjecture that he was only doing this for the money had been so callous on my part. Michael's pain, and my own stupidity, tore me wide open.

While David continued reading the article in silence, Michael's words replayed in my head with an agony that wrenched my soul. I had been so eager to accept David's side of the story over the years that I hadn't given any thought to what his actions had done to the person he abused. David may honestly have thought they had reconciled, but it was certainly not over for Michael. I reread the last few lines of the article where he stated that what ultimately made him come forward was how convinced he was that David was minimizing his actions. To Michael, it felt like the apology David had given all those years ago was a lie.

As I sat in silence trying to absorb this information, a new truth landed in the pit of my stomach: it was almost certain that David's life as a priest was over. I suspected, based on my own reaction, that hearing from the victim would make people more angry and less forgiving. There was already talk of the church considering a zero-tolerance policy, meaning that anyone who was credibly accused would be defrocked, no matter the circumstances.

I could feel David's eyes on me, but it was hard to look at him for fear my face would reveal my new perspective. Conflicting emotions were tearing me up. I was pissed at the church, sick about Michael, and sad for David all at the same time. He was a good man; I knew that better than anyone. He would never intentionally bring harm to someone, and I knew it pained him deeply when he contemplated the damage he had caused. They were both victims—Michael of David's actions, and David of the ridiculous church rules.

Finally, the silence was broken.

"What did you think?" I could hear the distress in his voice and I ached at what I would have to withhold from him. I couldn't speak of these new realizations with him now, not yet. Even with this latest information, my revulsion slowly turned to understanding for David. I knew why he had made such a horrible error; he was like an adolescent given a driver's license too young—bound to have a terrible accident. A week of horrendous decisions could forever rob him of the one thing he felt born to do. Could he ever rebound from this kind of loss? And it wasn't just his loss. David had always championed those that were excluded from the mainstream, especially those who were turned away from whatever spiritual practice they preferred. Gays and gender-variant people were only a few that he felt were barred from their rightful spiritual heritage. He was also an advocate for prisoners, the poor, and women who wanted to be ordained as ministers. Stripping him of his ability to serve was such a waste. And even though he had protected me through so much, there was no way for me to protect him now. That's what got to me the most. My heart was breaking for him. He was being publicly shredded and humiliated, and I could only help him by keeping his spirits hopeful and encouraging him. So that's what I did.

"I thought it was balanced and informative. Your story shines a spotlight on the hidden impact of celibacy, that's for sure, and it needs to come out." I put my hand on his thigh and leaned over to kiss him. "I'm so proud of you for standing up and doing the right thing."

16

Erased. 2004

The earthy smell of wet clay enveloped me, calming my jangled nerves. The tension in my body and mind was absorbed by the serene rotation of the pottery wheel as it spun around with a whisper. It was far better for me to have my hands in clay when I reflected on what was happening at home—it grounded me like nothing else. As I feared, things had become a shitshow for David. He was immediately yanked from public view. His forced leave meant he could no longer celebrate Mass or run the AIDS Ministry, which was closed down by a church administrator. Calls from former parishioners had ceased, and dinner invitations to their homes dried up. David's former life had been obliterated. As things dragged on, he fell into a depressing funk of despair. With nothing to do, David was home a lot more, becoming increasingly moody and possessive of my time, and it was suffocating me.

As I slowly shaped the clay into a bowl, the previous night crept into the edges of my mind. We had just watched the latest news story about the growing sex scandal. There was a tidal wave of public outcry about the mishandling by church officials of sexual abuse allegations happening all over the world. Priests were being kicked out in droves as the deepening scandal uncovered the sickening extent of the abuse the church had been covering up for decades. We had been in limbo since he was placed on administrative leave. David had petitioned the Archbishop to review his case, citing special circumstance because he had been successfully released for ministry by a therapist years ago. But he learned his request would have to be evaluated by the Vatican. Who knew how long that would take? The news reports did nothing to ease David's ongoing panic.

"I know I messed up, but I did everything that was asked of me. How long will this go on? What if I get permanently kicked out?" It was the same questions every night and I didn't know how much more I could take. It was gut wrenching to see him in so much pain, but the emotions and questions I had after reading about Michael kept banging around in my head. The pottery wheel was still spinning as the bowl was taking shape, but the rim was starting to wobble as his words rattled inside of me. I stopped the wheel and inhaled deeply. As my breath slowed, I concentrated on the comfort of having my hands in the wet clay. Then, I let the questions drift back into my mind. What on earth was going through David's mind that made him believe he could get away with such atrocious behavior? Why did he insist what he did wasn't sexual? It was a good thing he agreed to go into therapy, but his obedience to the church made no sense to me. When the bowl was completely shaped, I stopped the wheel and removed it, placing it on the rack to dry. I still needed answers, but I certainly couldn't ask David anything yet; he was simply too raw to talk about it. Still agonizing over these unanswered questions, I packed up and left the studio. As I was driving home, it hit me like a lightning strike: his journals. When this incident first came up years ago, he told me I could read the daily notes he had kept of his therapy sessions. I had no reason to read them at the time, but now I hoped they would contain the answers I was looking for.

Later that night after David was asleep, I tiptoed into the bedroom closet where he kept his journals. Pulling down the dusty briefcase from the shelf, I removed the thick folder and went out to settle into the living room. Taking a deep breath, I dove in. Hungrily sifting through the pages for anything that might help, I suddenly found it:

> *I realize I need to accept more responsibility for the harm I did to some kids by my sexual acting out. It still sticks in my throat to admit I hurt them. I'm thinking also of the seeming opportunism on the part of the young man who insisted on payment for damages. But the painful truth is that it was me who was the opportunist. I realize now that I betrayed his trust and exploited him. He had a right to compensation for the pain he endured.*

I read it. I read it again. His words slowly seeped into me. This was it. He knew. He *did* know that he had done wrong. This is exactly what I was looking for. Relief began to settle into me. He had taken ownership of what he had done to Michael, so why had he downplayed it later? When he first told me about this years ago, he probably thought he had told me enough. I could understand that. But why had he done the same thing with the reporter? I knew how badly he wanted to keep his job, so maybe that was why he minimized his story for the public. He thought this whole thing was behind him, but his choice not to fully own what he did had backfired. Michael may never have come forward if David had been more forthright in the first place. Feeling better, I went back to reading. After combing through several more pages, another section caught my eye:

> *I had a great conversation with another resident about my radical commitment to God and the absolute trust in God inherent in ordination and my religious vows. Absolute trust means to go where I am called, no matter how hard the circumstances. When I was asked to come to the treatment center, I reluctantly agreed because I wanted to be faithful to the church. They required something of me because of my offense that I found terribly painful and frightening, but I did it because my commitment requires obedience and trust. My trust in God is that somehow it will all work out.*

I was suddenly boiling with so much rage that I had to stifle my screams. My stomach filled with acid. Talk about misplaced loyalty! He thought if he stayed obedient to the church that everything would be fine, but there was nothing about this that was okay. His radical commitment is what caused him to sacrifice his humanity in the first place. I could hardly keep reading because I was so furious at the church. It was all well and good that David would submit to the treatment center, but it galled me that he was only there because the horrible policy of celibacy prevented him from having the kind of physical contact we all need. Like a lamb to the slaughter, the church had hooked him up to wires to prove he wasn't a pedophile, but when it showed he wasn't, they killed off his career anyway. What was the point of it all?

I kept poring over the pages, reading everything I could find about his struggles, his attempts to forgive himself, his thoughts on celibacy, and his raging anger at the church, which he had stifled for so long. I consumed everything I could—and then I got to the part about his torment around finding love:

> *If I fall in love, I fear that I will not experience the single-hearted joy and fulfillment from my life and ministry like I did before. Can I fulfill both needs, both dreams? I believe it can be done, but at times the pain of self-doubt is so intense. What do I do with the pain? I sit with it, pray with it, cry over it. I share it with friends and family. That usually brings me to a state of better well-being, but it doesn't remove the longing, which is a roaring, painful, empty place in my chest. Being in love and needing love are not easy experiences, but it is so much better to be walking around in the daylight on such things. These feelings are hard, but at least I know I am alive.*

My throat constricted as I digested his words. I realized now what a pressure cooker his life had been over the last decade; he was hoping that he had put the Michael thing behind him, he wanted to hold onto his priesthood, and at the same time he wanted the love and intimacy he desperately needed. My chest heaved with emotion as I processed all that he had sacrificed to be with me. It was so cruel that he had to choose at all. I had never fully realized the extent of any of these struggles. A surge of immense appreciation burst out of me. How perfectly mutual our love was. His unwavering care, the honesty and delight that he brought every day, was the salve that had kept me strong. It anchored both of us. My thoughts jumped to one of his first journal entries after arriving at the treatment center. He had expressed his vulnerability and fear over the reality that his life was completely in the hands of the church. He thought he had paid his penance and now he was here all over again. I finally understood.

I shut the journal and returned it to the briefcase, quietly replacing it on the shelf in the bedroom. As I crawled into bed and snuggled up to David, my body was filled with a renewed affection. No matter how long it would take to get out of the deep, dark tunnel we were in, I would stand by his side.

The church would likely forsake him, but I would not.

17

Near Catastrophe. 2004

"Nothing says old geezer like hearing aids," I ribbed David as we sat in the exam room waiting for the results from the hearing tests. He had been driving me crazy with his incessant 'what?' to everything I said, so I was thrilled when he finally agreed to get checked out.

David grinned. "I don't need hearing aids—you just have to stop talking like you have marbles in your mouth!" It was so nice to have him joking around. It had been over two years since the whole church thing went sideways and I was glad to have him back to normal. Our days had resumed a comfortable pace, which was so relaxing after the press had blown our lives apart. David had reverted to his delightful former self as we played the waiting game with the Vatican's decision. He was still on administrative leave, earning 60 percent of his former salary, so we had made the necessary financial adjustments. Most of his time was spent writing a spiritual blog with his thoughts on relevant Catholic teachings that inspired him, meeting primarily with gay people who appreciated his counsel about whether to stay with the church, and spending plenty of time with his mother going to movies and Mass.

"I need to show you what we found," the doctor said as he entered the exam room. He placed some film on the lightboard and pointed to a large opaque spot on the X-ray.

"What the hell is that?" I blurted out as I stared at the spot on his brain. The doctor had conducted a routine MRI as part of his hearing test, but having something wrong with his head was the last thing on our minds. David glanced at me but said nothing. We looked to the doctor expectantly.

"It's a brain tumor," he replied, "and it is much more dangerous than your hearing loss." I stopped breathing. David's face whitened with shock, and he stared at the doctor in disbelief. As the words 'brain tumor' careened around in my head, the doctor went on to tell us that there was, in fact, good news.

"If you hadn't come in for the hearing test, we would never have known about the tumor." Then he pointed to another spot below the white blob on the image. "The mass is situated on top of the optic nerve, which could lead to blindness if it moves or grows." I looked over at David, who was staring at the image, wordless. He turned his eyes in my direction, locking my gaze. Nothing needed to be said. My stomach tightened as the doctor kept talking.

"It is likely benign since you aren't having symptoms, but it still needs to come out. I know this is a lot to take in, but I can't stress enough the urgency of having it removed as soon as possible. Normally I would wait for several months and gauge the growth rate, but our test shows there is already pressure building on the optic nerve, so I think we should get it removed next week. It doesn't take much to disable your eyesight permanently." This last sentence came out without hesitation, as if to put the finest point possible on his argument.

We drove home in silence. How is one supposed to absorb that kind of news? I couldn't know everything David was feeling, but I was terrified of losing him. All that mattered to me was him getting through the surgery in one piece. Our lives had become so entangled with each other's and it was heart wrenching to imagine the possibility of him not being there. My mind shuffled through scenes of us together: at home, laughing with friends, in the car, running errands, at the movies. Instead of feeling happy, the memories brought on a withering sadness. I had never been alone. Without David, who was I? Then my mind suddenly switched to a fear I hadn't had in years. I was getting a disability income and standard Medicare insurance, but I was also paying for a secondary policy that covered the 20 percent that Medicare didn't pay for the exorbitant costs of the specialty medications I was taking. Living with David allowed me to afford it on my meager income.

By the time we got home, my mind was spinning out of control about both surgery and finances. Expecting to be dead by now, I had spent over 90 percent of my inheritance from Tom. We were cobbling together David's reduced income, my monthly disability, and whatever pottery sales brought in to pay the bills. If he were gone, his income would disappear—right along with my supplemental health insurance.

"Are you okay?" David asked. He had been surprisingly calm and seemingly unshaken since we got home, but I was freaked out, and it must have been written all over my face. There was nothing about any of this that was 'okay.'

"No, not really," I said. "The thought of losing you scares the hell out of me, and the practical stuff also has me worried sick." I felt selfish that I was making this about me when David was the one who had to go through such a dreadful surgery, but I also knew him—and he would want to know.

Tell me, David said without words. I took a deep breath to steady myself.

"My biggest fear is being unable to pay for health insurance. If I lose that, I'm a goner."

David rose from his chair and came over to sit beside me on the couch. "Don't worry," he said, putting his arm around me. "I'll talk to Mom and I'm sure she'll agree to cover your medical expenses if anything happens to me." I was so choked up that no words came out. "And besides, you'll inherit whatever I have," he went on to reassure me. "Don't worry; everything will work out." I nestled into his body and my anguish began to fade. Tears washed my eyes as his love poured over me.

We spent the week before surgery engrossed in all the contingency planning that had to be done, like setting up automatic house payments, getting bills paid, and letting people know what was going on. Once everything was complete, there was nothing to do but wait for the day of the operation to arrive.

"As much as I believe in an afterlife, I'm still pretty attached to this mortal coil," David told me the day before the surgery. He had been spending a lot of time contemplating his mortality, which wasn't unusual given his occupation, but I knew that, like me, he was also worrying about what might go wrong. The procedure itself was dangerous and gruesome. I flashed back to the conversation we had had with the surgeon.

"We use special medical saws to cut into the skull and open his head, but we have to be very careful. Since various nerves in the brain control lots of essential things, like keeping the heart beating and the lungs taking in oxygen, we have to avoid or reroute the nerves that keep the body functioning. Once we've done this, basically we pull apart the lobes of the brain, snip out the tumor, and then put it all back together." My stomach was doing somersaults. David's eyes were wide open. Jeez, it all sounded like science fiction to me, not to mention gory as hell. So many things could go wrong! I was grateful for modern medicine, but I couldn't shut out thoughts of the danger. What if he went into a coma? Had a stroke? Or died on the operating table trying to save his eyesight? Any number of things could go wrong, but for now all we could do was wait.

That night was a mixture of laughter and tears. We joked about the dirty trick the Universe had played on us: David was supposed to take care of me until I died, not the other way around.

"If you start drooling or shitting your pants, I'm out of here," I kidded, taking any opportunity to lighten the mood. Looking at him, I was reminded of our unlikely meeting twelve years ago, that fateful day when I walked into his office, still grieving Tom.

"I was just thinking about how much we've gone through together since we first met," I said, turning the conversation more serious, "and how incredible it has been to be with you at every step." Tears collected in my eyes and began to pool in his.

"It *is* incredible; I'd even say miraculous," he replied, smiling. "Do you remember that quote from Pope John Paul II I like so well?

That *the purpose of suffering is to release love?* Neither of us could have known how many painful turns our lives would take, but I believe our suffering has released into the world something bigger than us." It was true; we had both experienced traumas that nearly consumed us, yet healing could arise from the ashes of disaster. "I love you," he added, "and no matter what happens, know that you've changed my life in more ways than I could ever count." That's when I lost it. I pulled him close, hugging him tightly. I was incredibly lucky to have such a beautiful man to adore, and yet I might lose him, and I couldn't bear to think about it.

The next afternoon, in the lobby of Swedish Hospital, I waited for news. David had been in surgery for nearly six hours. His mom and a few friends were there. The surgical nurse reported every ninety minutes, and the next hour, the most technically difficult part of the procedure, was critical. We filled the time by reinforcing our confidence that he'd make it through. "He exercises and eats the right foods," his mom reminded us, likely trying to quell her own fears. Her husband had died the previous year and she depended on David as much as I did. I tried to remain calm, but my body felt rigid, masquerading as a protective shield.

Trying to engage with David's mother and his friends was exhausting any reserve I had. How would I react if the doctor came out with bad news? What about his mom; how would she react? It took everything I had to repel my thoughts of doom, imagining the first words that might come out of the doctor's mouth: I'm sorry, but we did everything possible. A horrible black dread came over me. I excused myself and made my way out of there. My pace quickened as I neared the door, the held-back feelings erupting the minute I hit the sidewalk. I found a bench and continued to sob until the tears turned into internal pleas of distress. How much more could I take? After losing Tom, making a fool of myself with the manic episode, nearly dying from cancer, and dealing with David's church mess, things had finally started to look up. I wanted to scream to the Universe: *Please, do not take David away from me!* After everything he had gone through, not to mention spending his life serving hundreds of people, this is what happens? He was a priest, for crying out loud; didn't that come with any perks? I was sputtering out of self pity and knew I had to pull myself together. I concentrated on slowing my breathing and forced myself to return to the waiting room. When I rejoined our group, the mood had definitely shifted. David's mom started talking as soon as she saw me.

"The nurse just came out and told us they finished and everything went really well." I began to breathe more easily as she shared the news. She beamed with hope, telling me her prayers had been answered. I didn't care who got credit; I was just glad he survived.

When the surgeon came out, he was all smiles. "The procedure could not have gone better. He's in stable condition and recovering. You can see him once they get him settled." It was like coming up for air; relief filling me with joy and my fear evaporating. We had dodged another bullet.

I grinned excitedly when I saw his eyes were wide open as I arrived at the ICU. The top of his head was covered with dressings and his face was swollen; tiny tubes were hanging from his headwrap.

"Hi, honey," I whispered. He glanced in my direction, expressionless. "You made it through!" I went on encouragingly. His face remained flat, yielding no recognition. "It's me, Steve." No reaction. He stared at me like I wasn't there.

A chill flashed up my spine as the blood drained from my face. I had been so relieved that he survived the surgery that I hadn't considered he wouldn't be back to normal. But now, as I took in his blank expression, other possibilities crowded my mind. Would he be brain-dead? Would he be like this from now on? Panic rippled through my body. I couldn't bear the thought of him not knowing who I was. Seeing him lying there, looking right at me without his usual tender smile, was like a dagger plunged into my heart.

As the doctor entered, I spun around to look at him, my eyes wide with fear. I tried to form the question, but the words were stuck in my throat. The doctor glanced at David and then back at me. "Don't worry," he said reassuringly, "everyone goes through this. Give him a couple of days. He'll be back."

18

Recovery and Release. 2004–2005

played the doctor's words over and over in my mind, "He'll be back, he'll be back, he'll be back." It was my ongoing mantra to assure myself that David's blank face and mute voice would not last.

The first three days felt like three weeks—there was no change in his demeanor. It was the fourth day when I walked in and immediately noticed a monumental difference. The tender bright gaze I had seen thousands of times whenever he looked at me was back. His eyes held mine and I saw a gleam of recognition that had been missing since the operation. My heart raced, and it took everything I had to keep from running over to his bed and throwing my arms around him. I refrained only because he was still so physically precarious. I grinned widely with anticipation, expecting him to speak, but I quickly realized that was wishing for too much. Still, something had definitely changed.

"Hi, dear," I said softly, moving toward his bedside and taking his hand. Waves of relief overtook me as he rasped out sounds that held a hint of my name. His face remained frozen, no smile or movement of his forehead or eyebrows, but the doctor had told me this was normal. I didn't care; at least I knew he was coming back to me.

By the end of the first week, David was moved from the ICU into a private room. I was grateful that the most critical part of this crisis, from a life-and-death perspective, was over. As he slowly emerged from his catatonic state, he was agitated. He was barking at everyone who came into the room. "Get out of here," he'd thunder at whichever unlucky nurse or technician happened to check on him. They remained calm, but I was distressed by his outbursts. Hearing him bark, "No!" when the nurses turned on the lights, took his blood pressure, or asked him too many questions made me cringe. I knew it was a combination of no sleep, pain, and the severing of his neural synapses during surgery. But it was hard to take in this new version of David.

By Day 10 after the surgery, David's mood had begun to lighten up. He had finally gotten some sleep, the pain was diminishing, and he was walking through the corridors with assistance. That evening, the doctor stopped by for his usual visit.

"I've got some good news," he announced. "You've been doing so well that we're going to let you out tomorrow." I saw the small grin break out on David's face as I felt a frown forming on mine. It was true that David had made some definite improvement, but he was a long way from independence. He would still need help dressing and bathing, preparing meals, and managing his medications. While his speech was improving, he wasn't talking much. A silent scream of protest rose in my throat, but David was already packing his nightstand, so I could hardly speak up. I frantically looked at David, then back at the doctor. Sensing my alarm, the doctor tried to reassure me.

"I know it seems daunting, but you'll do fine. He's not as fragile as he might look. You can call us day or night and we'll send someone over right away." I glanced again at David and realized I had to do this. Not only because he wanted it, but because he would do it for me.

When we entered the house the following day and began the slow, careful ascent up the stairs, my heart raced with fear that he would fall over backwards and split his head wide open. When I managed to get him safely into bed, the thumping in my chest slowed. As he sat down, I removed his clothes and got him settled comfortably. Then I propped him up in a seated position, his back against the headboard and pillows stuffed on both sides of his body, as instructed by the doctor, to keep fluids from building up in his skull. I was too afraid to ask why this was important, but figured it shouldn't be too hard to do. David was so exhausted from the interrupted sleep and noisy environment of the hospital that he immediately fell into a deep, snoring slumber.

I was way too nervous to leave him right away, so I pulled up a chair next to the bed and watched him sleep. I couldn't peel my eyes off his forehead where fifty-six staples, Frankenstein-like, were sunken into his scalp along the hairline from ear to ear. Adding to the beat-up look were the puffy purple-yellow bags hanging under his bloodshot eyes. He was wearing a 'cranny cap,' a lightweight cotton fabric hat that covered the top of his head. It hid the healing surgical incisions and kept him warm. Taking in his battered head and body made me reflect on how he must have felt while at the same bedside readying my puke pails and wondering if I was going to make it. Was he scared for me, like I was for him now?

The next morning when I saw him lying flat on the bed, I gasped. The doctor's imperative about keeping him upright rang through my head and I kicked myself for sleeping in the other room.

"Were you in this position all night?" I said, biting the inside of my lip to keep from shouting. It took every ounce of self-restraint I possessed to keep from racing over and pushing his body into an upright position.

He flashed me an annoyed look. "I don't know; I was sleeping." I knew better than to push it, so I let it go and helped him sit up, propping the pillows back into place and getting him resituated. His cranny cap had fallen off during the night and when I looked at his uncovered head, I was shocked. I thought I saw the top of his head moving. Not wanting David to sense my horrified chill, I nonchalantly stepped closer and pretended I was putting on his cap when I saw it move again. The top of his head was slushy, like liquid pulsating under his skin. His skull looked like a waterbed. I touched it lightly but immediately jerked back my hand at the unexpected feel of plastic wrap over water instead of a hard bony surface. Oh my god, this cannot be normal. Why did they think I could be home alone with him?

"Is everything okay?" David asked, his voice hanging in the air.

I knew I had to give him an answer, so I chose my words carefully to avoid startling him. "Well, it's a little soft." I whipped out my phone and called the nurse.

"Did he sleep upright through the night?" Her words hit me like a personal accusation. How could I have let that happen? Once again I chastised myself for sleeping in the other room. My face turned hot with embarrassment. I had screwed up.

"No. When I found him this morning he was lying completely flat on the bed," I replied, forcing myself to spit out the truth. "Is he in any danger?"

"No, you don't need to worry. This happens to most people," she assured me. "Once he sits up, the fluid will drain back into his facial tissue." My pulse began to slow back down to normal and after relaying the message to David and shaking off the 'yuck factor,' I relaxed. Never having seen such a gruesome aftermath of surgery, I was relieved it wasn't something to worry about.

The next several days were slow and routine: help him out of bed, escort him to the bathroom, get him dressed, make food, then settle him onto the sofa and sit with him. I would check his incision twice daily for redness and try to assess the level of wateriness to firmness. According to the doctor, the skull sections that were separated during surgery slowly stitch themselves back together. It was astounding what the body could do! There still wasn't much talking with David, but there were days when his personality would poke through. I was putting on his socks one morning when I decided to see if he would rise to my teasing. Knowing how fastidious he was about wearing matching socks, I started putting on a slightly mismatched pair and waited. It didn't take long before he frowned at me with a clear message on his face: take it off. Yep, he was still in there!

I was slowly adapting to my role as caregiver, but what I hadn't anticipated was the exhausting job of also being gatekeeper. As soon as I got David home, the calls started pouring in from people wanting to see him. Many of the calls were from friends and former parishioners who meant well but had no idea of the reality. His mother and close friends were the only ones allowed over for a while, but their frequent visits and phone inquiries exhausted him, so random drop-ins were out. On top of that, I was concerned about how David would act around others. He wasn't his priestly self. His answers were short and sharp and, while I was used to it, I knew it could sound offensive. My answer became like a broken record. "He's doing better every day, but is not yet well enough to have visitors." I did my best to strike a balance between pleasant and forceful.

When I wasn't playing David's phone receptionist, I would ask him for an update on how he was feeling. We called it the organ recital: talk about what ails you. It reminded me of what he had done when I was sick; several times a week we reviewed my physical symptoms to make sure he knew everything. I marveled at how the tables had turned—now he was having health problems and I gladly stepped up.

Over the next few months, his vigor and vocabulary slowly returned. I was so relieved, as the months felt like years with his progress of recovery being so slow. When we were finally able to start taking incrementally longer walks, not only did his physical strength improve but we were getting back to our normal way of communicating. He was also joining me each morning for meditation, something that was new for him. While David was an avid Catholic, I was a practicing Buddhist. Once death had landed squarely in my living room after losing Tom, I had begun searching for ways to calm the growing fear of my own dying. The version of

Christianity that I had grown up with did nothing to comfort me. After reading *The Power of Now*, by Eckhart Tolle, a new way of looking at myself and spirituality took hold. I no longer believed in the type of god that was drummed into my head as a child—the ultimate arbiter of my fate. The liberation this provided struck me deeply, and it provoked lively conversations between David and me about the differences in the two forms of spirituality. We used different words to essentially describe the same thing. Whereas he offered reverence to God, I used words like Buddha or the Universe. I didn't know whether it was because of the meditating, but it was obvious David was much calmer, peaceful even. He hadn't mentioned anything about the priesthood or the church since the surgery, so I was starting to get curious. We were on one of our walks around the neighborhood when I decided to bring it up.

"You haven't talked about the church drama in a while. Why is that?"

I wondered whether this question had been a good idea, but before I could worry about it, he spoke. "I guess the easiest way to answer is a little thing called Life and Death—both have been weighing on my mind ever since the surgery. Having my life threatened with that brain tumor has really opened my eyes about what's important—and getting back into a broken church has lost its appeal." Wow. That was shocking to hear. I stayed quiet to encourage him to keep talking. "When I speak to my oldest friends who are still priests, listening to all the bullshit they have to put up with now is ridiculous. Why should I subject myself to that again? Most of them are burnt out and counting the days till retirement. I've been fighting to hold on to this precious vocation, but I think it's been out of desperation to have things go back to the way they were. I've realized that's nothing but a fantasy."

I was stunned by this 180 degree change. We seemed to be seeing the church in a similar way now; maybe that brain surgery did more than just save his eyesight! I could feel a smile begin to break out on my face. He had definitely turned a corner.

Still savoring his words as we got home and sat down in the living room for coffee, I picked up the conversation again.

"Have you thought about what you might do instead of being a priest?"

"Not exactly, but I've spent time dissecting what I loved about the church, and it always boils down to serving people. I can still do that in another capacity. I don't know what that will look like, but I'm sure we can figure it out together." He reached over to take my hand and we sat together quietly. This was the David I had fallen in love with, the man who creates his own destiny after being forged in the furnace of life's inevitable difficulties. I broke the silence with a question that was weighing on me.

"But what if the Vatican decides you can stay a priest? We still don't know what their final decision will be." I was a bit afraid to ask this, fearing it might suddenly make him more tentative about his decision.

"First off, my priest friends in high places are sure they've already decided—there's not a chance in hell I'm going to get any special treatment. Zero tolerance is all they are talking about because it makes it easy for the Vatican to look tough in the public's view. If they make exceptions, it just opens them up to criticism. They don't give a shit about me; they just want to put this behind them."

He had clearly given this a great deal of thought; he spoke with determination and resolve. My heart began to beat wildly as inside I cheered for him. "Secondly, even with everything that's happened, I'm grateful for my time as a priest and know that when they kick me out it will never negate the positive experience." There was my triumphant David—he could get to the goodness in just about anything. He paused for a moment as he turned to face me, nothing but affection painting his face. "And most importantly, it's been such a relief not having the church breathing down our necks and forcing us to stay quiet about our relationship. I've loved that." He leaned in and wrapped his arms around me, and I nearly melted. To hear him say these words was an answer to a long-held dream. Even though we were living together, we were still forced to be careful what we said to people. We didn't dare divulge our shared address to the wrong person, so it still felt like we were living in the closet. It was stifling in there, so the idea that we could be free of all that was as if a symphony orchestra had just taken up residence inside, the sounds of beautiful music overwhelming everything else.

It was just a few days later when the call came from the Archbishop. It was a short conversation. "It's done, I'm out," David said, hanging up the phone. "It's finally over." The tone of his voice communicated his relief.

I pulled him into a hug. "This is the day we've been waiting for," I whispered, "It's time to start our new life."

19

Newly Committed. 2006

The comfortable silence in the living room was pierced by the rustling of the newspaper as David flipped the page. We were enjoying a leisurely morning, and I was ruminating about the change in the atmosphere at home since the church no longer had an influence on our personal lives. "Doesn't it feel strange?" I said after downing my morning coffee. "After all those years of having to maintain a veil of secrecy around our relationship, now we can do whatever we want." David put down the paper and smiled big in response.

"It is strange, yes, and wonderful too." He put his finger up and said he'd be right back, then scurried off to the bedroom. When he returned to the living room, he had one hand behind his back. "It's wonderful because I finally get to ask the question I've wanted to ask you for years." A surge of pure love swelled up inside, my eyes glistening as it dawned on me what he was about to say. Before I could respond, he knelt down on one knee. I choked up, both stunned and thrilled, watching David through tear-filled eyes open a ring box. "Will you marry me?" he asked softly. Every part of my body screamed yes. After he slipped the engagement ring on my finger, I was eager to make it happen.

This was the day I'd dreamt about for years. It was in my nature to want to be in a committed relationship—and to me that meant marriage. It was what I had hoped for with Tom, but I had had to throttle back my marriage desires when I learned he was skeptical of serious commitment after being burnt by a former lover. It wasn't until he was nearing death that Tom was able to speak of his love for me, admitting the mistake he had made by keeping me at a distance. It was devastating for both of us to realize it was too late to do anything about it. David and I were madly in love from the start, but that damn priest thing was in the way. While we had talked about the possibility of marriage, it wasn't feasible until his priesthood came to an end. Now that I had a ring on my finger, I was eager to make it happen. Like other gay couples who were making their own ceremonies, we weren't going to let the laws of Washington that prevented gay marriage keep us from celebrating our union. We set a date for March, just six weeks away. We didn't want anyone else to perform the ceremony; David knew what to do. We wanted to make it a small, intimate affair at our home with family and close friends, but it also had to be spectacular. David got busy putting together the ceremony and ritual elements; I designed the invitations and figured out the refreshments.

When the day arrived, I felt like a nervous bride, pinching myself to make sure I wasn't hallucinating the whole thing. We had decorated our home sparingly but tastefully. Twinkling lights adorned a simple arbor we had constructed as a backdrop for our wedding vows. A friend had decked out our round wooden dining table with a floral centerpiece surrounded by delicious platters of food.

Once the guests arrived, David and I sat on separate high-backed stools under the archway at one end of our living room. Looking out at our guests seated in semi-circle rows, the beauty of this gathering rained down on me. The last fourteen years of our lives had been a cyclone of love and loss, and the select group of people in attendance had been there to witness most of it. They supported us without ever questioning our commitment to each other. We were eager to make this official proclamation, witnessed by those who had been asked to keep our long-held secret. My heart swelled as David stood up, his hands spread open in the classic priestly gesture as he welcomed our guests with opening remarks.

"Maybe you noticed in the invitations that we didn't call this a wedding? That was because it would have been the longest engagement in history." He smiled as everyone laughed. "We met in 1992 and within no time were living together like it was the most natural thing to do. And for us it was. It may have appeared to be a hasty decision, but boy has it ever worked out!" More chuckles came from our friends.

David stopped speaking and took on a more serious demeanor, readying himself to start the ceremony. While this may not have been an official Catholic wedding, David was determined to use many of the traditional components that held special meaning for him. He began to sing *a cappella* "Gloria," a classic opening hymn. I closed my eyes and imagined his voice resonating beautifully in a large cathedral, something I had heard many times. When my eyes opened, I noticed others joining in, most of whom were Catholic and knew the words by heart. My chest heaved with emotion—it was actually happening! We wanted to incorporate each of our individual styles, so when he finished, he nodded that it was my turn. I chose a more secular song, "Come What May," from our favorite musical, *Moulin Rouge*. The movie, starring Nicole Kidman and Ewan McGregor, focuses on the deep love and loss of the main characters, and it resonated deeply with both of us. I took a deep breath in and then slowly exhaled, looked over at David smiling, and sang from my heart. When I got to the lyrics of the chorus, I struggled to keep my composure:

> *Suddenly the world seems such a perfect place*
> *Suddenly it moves with such a perfect grace*
> *Suddenly my life doesn't seem such a waste*
> *It all revolves around you*
>
> *Come what may*
> *Come what may*
> *I will love you*
> *Until my dying day*

When I finished, there wasn't a dry eye in the house. David was glowing; I didn't think I'd ever stop smiling at him. Once the euphoria settled, David took the lead on the next part.

"When we first met, my life had recently been turned upside down, and when it finally righted itself, I was an out-of-the-closet gay priest. I was determined to find love, even though it felt nearly impossible. Who would be interested in dating me?" He looked at me lovingly and said, "Just when I was about to give up hope, Steve appeared in my office." He took my hand in his, capturing my gaze. "He was emotionally intelligent, incredibly brave, and grieving. I was so moved by his personal story of losing his partner, Tom, and

143

how he was handling his own health crisis. He was determined to live his life as fully as possible. We had that in common from the start; both of us were looking to rebuild our lives. It boggles my mind at the odds of us even meeting. Talk about a heavenly intervention," he finished, getting more laughter. I nodded in agreement, still believing Tom had something to do with it.

David's words took me right back to that fateful day, so it was easy to get started on my part. "When I met this man, my life had been turned upside down too. I felt like it was over for me, thinking it was just a matter of time before I followed Tom. David just listened at first, and that would have been enough, but then he started talking about hope and encouraging me to stay strong when everything appeared bleak. It was surprising how desperately I needed to hear those words. Speaking with such vulnerability showed me what it meant to have an empathetic listener. He held space for me to examine everything I had been through, with zero judgement, while offering the wisdom I needed at that moment." Several heads nodded; his remarkable gift had been experienced by most of them. "It was pretty hard not to fall in love with someone like that," I exclaimed, smiling big at him. We let a few moments of silence pass to bring that segment to a close.

My hands trembled; it was time to say our vows. It was this part of a wedding that always elicited such powerful emotions in me. Every ceremony I attended as a young adult had made me blubber when it came time to exchange rings and state those two incredible words, 'I do.' Part of it was the sadness I felt in being gay and thinking it was never going to happen for me, but I also loved the romantic idea of loving someone until the end. It was this kind of commitment

I wanted to make. Now, as we took our positions facing each other, it was finally coming true. David whispered, "Here we go" as we intertwined our hands. I felt like there was no one in the room but us. Our surroundings fell away as we gazed into each other's eyes. As we recited the words that promised our lifelong commitment 'in sickness and in health, until death do us part,' my mind flashed back to his tumor, my cancer, and all the love and laughter we had shared. It dawned on me that we had already been living these vows. When it came time to exchange rings and declare 'I do' to each other, I was so giddy I could hardly get out the words. We didn't have to wait for anyone to tell us to kiss, so we locked our lips together as soon as we had each spoken those magic words. Everyone stood and applauded enthusiastically.

* * *

We quickly settled into our new life. It was an exciting fresh start and we wanted to take some time to enjoy it. The work thing would eventually need to be figured out but, in the meantime, we sold our Capitol Hill condo for a less expensive place in the South end of Seattle and tightened our belts. There was no money for an expensive honeymoon, so instead we chose staying close to home and hosting dinners for our friends. One of our staple meals was a simple dish of kalamata olives with chopped artichoke hearts and garlic sautéed in olive oil and tossed with spaghetti. It was the first meal David had prepared for me, and we loved telling the story about how impressed I was with his cooking—even though I learned later it was the only dish he knew how to make.

We had just wrapped up enjoying the famous dinner dish with Gary, the friend who had introduced me to David, when he proposed an idea. "It's so much fun to just hang out, why don't you guys come to our place for the entire weekend? I know money is tight, and it would be fun to just chill at our house for a few days. Think of it as a staycation; you'd be at our place instead of sitting home." It was easy to say yes, so we planned the first one for the following weekend and Gary announced the ground rules. "The main thing is that we stay in our pajamas all weekend—that means no leaving the house for anything. I'll do all the cooking, so just bring your snacks and beverages," he instructed. Sounded like heaven to me. When we arrived on Friday night, the aroma of a sage and garlic pot roast was the first thing that pleasantly lit up our senses. Gary and his partner Kevin were expert cooks, so we knew the food was going to be scrumptious. Dinner included roasted rosemary potatoes and grilled asparagus, followed by peach cobbler with vanilla ice cream. After eating, we changed clothes and waddled into the family room to watch *Auntie Mame* with Rosalind Russell—one of our favorite movies. The next two days were nothing but lazy mornings, slow days talking and laughing about the stupidest things, eating and taking naps whenever we felt like it, watching movies or curling up with a book. We were pleasantly stranded with nothing to do but lounge around and be together. When it came time to leave, we vowed to start up what would become a tradition: Pajama Party Weekends.

We didn't know what the future held, but right then, everything felt new and magical. The excitement was hard to contain as the world took on a sparkling new appearance. We were finally done hiding.

20

Divine Intervention. 2007-2008

David was bursting with excitement as he came barreling out of the bedroom. "You won't believe who just called me—the executive director of St. Vincent de Paul!" I had no idea why this was such good news, but I didn't have to wait long for him to explain. "He just asked me to come in for an interview. He told me he had heard one of my sermons years ago, and he thinks he might have a job for me."

Lucas Anderson, the executive director he spoke to, was impressed by how David preached about the poor and disadvantaged, which was the community to which that organization provided services. Relief washed over me as David's excitement grew about this prospect. To say that he was desperate for work was the understatement of the year. But it wasn't as if he hadn't been trying. After enjoying a few months of down time after our honeymoon, he had started pounding the pavement for work. He reached out to his nun friends first, who had an open position as the manager of one of their low-income housing buildings, but it had fallen through. Next, he tried his hand at providing spiritual consulting services. I helped him set up a website to offer workshops and weddings to the public, but that quickly fizzled out because he wasn't good at marketing himself. Then, he reached out to his network of former parishioners to offer wedding, funeral, and spiritual counseling services, but they were accustomed to getting priestly services for free, so that didn't work out either.

And it wasn't just David at a crossroads. Over the previous year, I had noticed a growing ache in my feet and hands, which ended up being diagnosed as hereditary osteoarthritis. I had just turned 46 and had no idea how bad it might get. Would I end up in a wheelchair like my Great Uncle Bill did in his thirties? Pottery required too much lifting and dexterity for someone with arthritis, and my heart sank when I realized I was going to have to let go of the one thing that had long been my haven.

I tried to stay positive, but the truth was that we both had hit a wall: this was David's first—and uncertain—job prospect, and I could not continue as a potter. What were we going to do? It was hard to imagine how we would be able to make it with so few options. Money was getting tighter. As time flew by, my worry grew.

David kept my hopes up. "Listen, I know things are uncertain right now, but let's not forget how much we've been through. We've dealt with brain surgery, cancer, and our friends dying too young from AIDS. Hell, at least we're still here." He was right, of course. It was important to stay focused on the big picture. After pulling me into an embrace, he whispered into my ear, "And the best thing is that we have each other. That's a lot to be grateful for." His reassurance never failed to dispel my fear.

Despite reason to be optimistic, David was nervous when it came time for the interview with Lucas from St. Vincent de Paul. "Don't worry, you'll do fine," I said, straightening his tie. "Just be yourself. Remember, he called you. He already thinks you're awesome." David relaxed and headed out the door smiling.

After he left, I sent out positive vibes to the Universe—visualizing that he was doing well at the interview. I had good reason to feel confident: St. Vincent de Paul was a Catholic organization not officially tied to the church, so they wouldn't need approval from the Vatican to hire him. Even though I was feeling positive, I was still on pins and needles when David rushed through our door with a big smile on his face. "I got the job!" he nearly shouted. "Lucas was nothing but supportive of my efforts to restart my career after the ouster and felt strongly that everyone deserves to have a job, no matter what. When he offered me the position to answer phones in their call center, I nearly cried." David gave me a long hug and was choked up with delight.

He started the following week, and his passion for the job soon dominated our dinner conversation. He relayed details about the callers and the difficulties of their lives. Everyone he spoke to was dealing with some major crisis, like needing money to avoid eviction or to feed their kids. "It's hard to imagine the kinds of struggles they endure, so it's humbling to help them in some way," David said as he took a bite of his dinner. "I feel like I'm back to being a priest!" I was happy for him, but I was also spiraling with angst and confusion not knowing what to do with myself. Once the pottery studio was closed, my days were wide open, and I missed the routine and comfort of working with clay. I spent more time meditating and being still, which helped momentarily settle the uncertainty I was feeling. *It's not about the future; it's about right now,"* I kept telling myself. Yet my mind would easily jump back onto its worn track of negative self-talk, and those moments of inspired stillness would collapse. Having no sense of direction made it nearly impossible for me to stay optimistic.

One night several weeks into his job, David's daily gushing about his work turned to the food bank that was located on site. "You wouldn't believe this place. Three hours before they open, there's a line a block long. Sometimes I'll help on the food line during my breaks, and it's remarkable to see the people who come in—not at all who you might imagine." I knew David had a soft spot for people in need, and it was heartwarming to hear him tell stories of those he met there. "There's this older woman, Lily, who comes every week. She takes two buses and walks six blocks to get there. She always has a smile on her face and when she told me recently that she was eighty-seven, I was floored. She's my mother's age and it made me choke up to think about it."

These stories began to pique my interest. I started asking David all sorts of questions about where the food came from, how many hours they were open, and who the staff was.

"You should go down and meet with them. I'm sure they'd love to tell you all about it. I know they are always looking for volunteers." Something sparked inside me.

A few days later I was meeting with Mike, the manager, learning about the program and the volunteer positions they had available. It was pretty amazing what they were doing in just two three-hour open periods a week—feeding one hundred families each day. The Buddhist in me was looking to serve others, so it was easy to picture myself there. Within minutes of declaring my interest, I had an application in my hand. As I filled it out, he told me about some idiosyncrasies of the place.

"You won't believe it until you see it," Mike said with a grin, "But I kid you not that when the doors are flung open, the throng of people that comes running in is crazy!" It sounded perfect. I started the following week.

I was instantly hooked. The people I worked with, both staff and volunteers, were welcoming, and it felt good to be around them. Plus, the people who came in for food all had their own unique charm. Having worked in isolation as a potter had made me forget how much I enjoyed the conviviality of others. At the start of my first day, we packed grocery bags with food collected from various sources. Each bag contained a box of cereal, a bag of frozen corn or peas, and other staples like flour, beans, and milk. Two-day-old pastries were popular, as were the piles of bread. We'd pack a hundred bags with the items and get the tables set up. The public arriving was both exhilarating and heart-wrenching.

Mike was right about a stampede, but it only happened on the days we had fresh vegetables. Dozens of older women, and a few men, made a beeline for the produce, jostling each other. They took as much as they could stuff into their bags; the table was stripped bare in minutes. The desperation of it all made it hard to watch. Then things got much calmer. A line formed and folks would come to a row of tables to get their pre-packed grocery bag, then the pastries and bread they wanted. People were friendly, talkative, and full of gratitude; I hadn't expected it to feel so good to be on the giving side. My three hours went by lightning fast—and by the time we closed the doors, my head was filled with all sorts of ideas to make the place better. I had forgotten how much I loved working. It reminded me of my early working days as a manager at McDonald's and later at the Four Seasons Hotel. I was a natural-born leader, and all my instincts were kicking in at the food bank. Within a few months, I was recruiting and training new volunteers, designing flyers, and helping with other managerial tasks.

Now, instead of being on the listening end of David talking about his day, I was the one dominating the dinner conversation. My head was overflowing with ideas to improve the food bank operation and I couldn't stop talking about it.

"We need to get serious about controlling the influx of people when we open the doors; it's chaotic and dangerous." I'd prattle on about creating directional signage and figuring out a way to stop the line jumpers. "I'm also thinking about a numbering system to keep order." David sat back, smiling as he listened to me ramble on and on. As soon as I took a breath to get some air, he jumped in. "This is great. Before you know it, you'll be running the place."

It had crossed my mind that the position could turn into a part-time job. I had been worried about my lack of recent work experience, and this seemed like the perfect way to get it. But, just as my enthusiasm began to rise, a familiar black cloud invaded my psyche—the dilemma of collecting disability insurance. It seemed that I could make a meaningful career but, if I started working, I'd lose my disability insurance and besides, a part-time job wouldn't offer health insurance. Even if I could get employer insurance to replace disability, I still didn't know whether I could keep up with a full-time job. If I got sick and had to quit, I'd need to start all over again applying for disability. How would I manage while I awaited approval—with $8,000 needed for my monthly drugs just to stay alive. We had enough to pay the usual monthly living expenses, but these exorbitant pharmaceutical costs could bankrupt us.

Even as the old stuck feeling gripped me, I was determined to make my new job prospect work. It had been a few years since I had looked into the rules about going off disability, and when I researched it again, I hit paydirt. I discovered a new program that blew me away. I kept reading it over and over because it seemed too good to be true, but there it was: a nine-month trial work period in which one could earn an unlimited amount without losing disability benefits. After that, one could decide whether they could physically keep up with the job. If yes, they would lose monthly disability income, but—here was the kicker—could keep Medicare health insurance for eight more years, no matter what. I cried out, elated. It was unbelievable! It was like a get-out-of-jail-free card.

I pitched my part-time job idea to Lucas and he jumped on it, giving approval on the spot. "They are going to be so glad they hired you," David exclaimed when I shared the great news that evening. "You're going to turn that place on its head." This part-time job at the food bank felt monumental. Over the next several months, I tore into the details of the operation and started suggesting changes, much to the delight of Mike and Lucas. And it was just in the nick of time as it turned out. The year was 2008 and the recession was hitting, so the food bank went from serving two hundred families per week to a thousand. It was insane how fast things changed. Crowd control was our biggest issue—the throngs of people continually had to be monitored. We installed portable stanchions to keep people lined up and contained. But instead of turning it into a policing situation, we had volunteers serving coffee and tea to people waiting in line. They got to know them, which greatly reduced the friction that sometimes flared up when no one was watching.

About six months in, I was called in to Lucas's office. I had no idea what he wanted, and when I saw Rena, the new human resources consultant, in his office, my head swarmed: Was I getting a raise or had I done something wrong? I knew she handled staffing issues and worked closely with Lucas on all things related to managing employees. I had met her a few months earlier when she was brought in to strengthen the employee and volunteer handbooks. She interviewed me about the volunteer recruitment I had done at the food bank. I thought we had hit it off.

"Everything you said you were going to do, you did," Lucas said, "and the food bank has been running better than it ever has." Rena was nodding in agreement. My shoulders relaxed and I stopped fretting.

"We've been impressed by how fast and thoroughly you've improved the volunteer program," Rena added, jumping into the conversation. "You have the right mix of skills and personality for a job we have in mind." She looked over at Lucas, who nodded for her to continue. My insides were shaking. "We'd like you to expand those volunteer recruitment efforts to the administrative offices and our five thrift stores throughout the city." I was speechless, floored by the scope of the job and stunned with excitement by the opportunity. As she spoke on about the specifics, it was all I could do to keep from breaking down into a mush-ball of tear-filled gratitude.

The years of self-doubt about whether I would ever work again had proved groundless and, without the risk of losing health insurance, I had a chance to start over. "So, to be clear," she went on, "We'd like to offer you a full-time job, with benefits. Are you interested?" It was as if I were just handed a winning lottery ticket. Of course I was interested! It took all the self-control I possessed to keep from jumping up and kissing both of them.

Instead, I replied without hesitation, "Absolutely. When can I start?"

21

Temporary Insanity. 2009 – 2010

S ome couples might feel strained working at the same place, but David was genuinely excited for me. At sixty-six, David's work life was nearing its end, while mine was just taking off. No one knew better what a struggle I'd gone through to get there. "It's incredible what you've accomplished in such a short time," he gushed every chance he got. " I'm so proud of you!"

Our evening ritual of debriefing the day remained in full swing, with talk about our jobs at St. Vincent de Paul still consuming much of the evening airtime. David had become manager of the call center, and the volunteer coordinator position I held for six months had morphed into a human resources job. We'd go to our respective offices in the morning and often have lunch at the same time. Getting up and going to work together felt wonderfully routine.

Not long after my promotion, a major change in leadership occurred. Lucas retired and a new executive director was hired. Ted was a tall man with thinning red hair and a graying goatee, a military retiree. Although he and his wife were longtime Catholics, it didn't take long to discover that he, too, was skeptical of the church, so we got along easily. He knew all about David's history and that we were a couple, and he thought it was great.

"As far as I'm concerned, it's none of the church's damn business," he said. My thoughts exactly. His personality and energy invigorated me as he began to shift organizational priorities. His ideas included taking better care of employees, which was especially exciting because that was my new area of responsibility and I'd have a key stake in making it happen. Meeting together in his office during his first weeks, I was thrilled and nearly disbelieving to be there. He made it clear from the start that I would be his right-hand person. Ted told me, "I know you are new to human resources and your experience is limited, but that's exactly the kind of person I like to work with. I'll show you what I know and give you the authority to make your own decisions."

There was a strong magnetism about Ted that drew me in. I liked it every time he asked for help. Before long, I was serving unofficially as his executive assistant, assisting with technology questions and proofreading his documents. As we began to meet with staff and learn about some of their challenges, he would tell me about employees he wanted to promote or terminate. He would confide in me about sensitive matters and it gave me great pleasure to be a trusted insider. There were several directors that reported to him, most of whom he thought were useless. There was one in particular, Robert, whom he especially despised. "He comes into my office and talks to me like I need his counsel, but he's an idiot," Ted would tell me in private. It felt amazing to be a part of his inner circle, one of his closest workplace confidantes. He saw leadership qualities in me that I had recognized years ago. He had taken me under his wing and was molding me into an executive leader, and that felt pretty damn good!

Ted also stoked my desire to do my best work, so I was determined to do things by the book. That meant making sure everyone was following the rules, including David, which sometimes caused us to butt heads. The discord usually involved him not wanting to discipline his employees, so he would sometimes neglect to document errors they had made. When I reminded him how important this was, he was usually pretty compliant, but every now and then he'd push back in defense of the employee or become annoyed when I pointed out something he missed.

"That's just administrative bullshit," was his favorite reply. His irritation never lasted long, though, and we'd move on.

There was a comfort in the routine of our days. After our evening discussions, we'd have dinner, walk Jetta, our newly-adopted miniature schnauzer, and settle down to either read or watch television. On weekends, we did the usual Saturday errands of a working couple, like grocery shopping and paying bills. But on Sundays, without fail, David would take his mother to church, followed by brunch, a movie, and then dinner. Before I started working, I would usually join them for the movie and dinner, but it was different now. Weekend time was a precious commodity for recharging my battery, and I relished the time for myself. David understood.

Life was going so well that I hardly thought about AIDS anymore. It had become ordinary and routine to swallow fourteen pills twice a day. Sometimes I'd wonder how my body was able to process the sheer volume of chemicals I had ingested for the past seventeen years; it was a miracle I could still stand upright. The drugs allowed what AIDS stood for me now: survival among the living. It was astonishing how different things had become. The constant stress of watching friends die and wondering who was next went by the wayside.

While my health remained stable, I still had to visit the doctor every six months for a routine prescription drug review. On one such visit, Dr. Meredith hit me with unexpected news. "I've decided to retire," she said. My mouth dropped open. Before I could launch a flurry of questions, she went on. "Insurance companies have become such a burden to making decisions about patient care that it's gotten to be too much." As she spoke, panic seized me. I needed to find a new doctor. Having been her patient since the beginning of AIDS, I had grown to trust her with my life. How could I possibly switch to someone else? She must have noticed my alarm. "Try not to worry. I have someone in mind that I feel would be a good match for you. He's gay, has been an AIDS doctor for years, and has plenty of patients in a similar health situation. You'll be in good hands, I promise."

Despite Dr. Meredith's assurances, I was nervous. But when I met Dr. Peterson the next week, I felt I was in the presence of an old soul. He had a long graying beard, wire-framed glasses, and piercing eyes. His soft words and kind face were draped with a humility that came from witnessing hundreds of young men die. I had heard of him off and on over the years as something of a legend in the eyes of those he had brought back from the brink of death.

After some pleasant small talk, the doctor got right to business.

"I've reviewed the files your doctor sent over, including your medication history. It looks like the AIDS treatment you've been on has kept you alive, but it may be time to consider a new regimen." This was something Dr. Meredith and I had begun to discuss over the past few years, but I was reluctant to change something that was working. When I expressed this to the doctor, he had a clear retort.

"I would disagree that it's working. Your viral load has never been completely undetectable, and there are newer medications that would very likely achieve that." He added that the new class of drugs had fewer side effects and was more effective at keeping the virus at bay. He went on to describe that the latest class of AIDS antiviral drugs were much better and I'd likely notice the difference right away. He spoke with such authority that I let my guard down as I took it in that maybe this new doctor would be fine.

It had been one month since starting the new antiviral regimen, and my body was still adjusting to it. Nausea and headaches were the main side effects so far. Dr. Peterson told me this was normal and not to worry, but when I woke up one morning with a rash, I freaked out. It was a lot like the one I had years ago that spread over my entire body and itched like mad. I immediately called the doctor and he prescribed Prednisone. A little alarm bell sounded in my head: Wasn't that the same medication that caused the first manic episode? But I told myself the odds of that happening again were pretty remote. I was sure my doctor knew what he was doing and I wanted to get past this rash so it wouldn't interrupt my work. It began to fade after a few days on the steroid. Plus, I was feeling really good and a lot more energized. I took advantage of this by working late into the night, studying up on human resources and refining our policies. I ignored distracting thoughts of what else might be happening.

"It's pretty late; when are you coming to bed?" David asked, getting up at midnight to find me in the bedroom we used as an office. Since starting back to work over a year ago, I had gotten into David's routine of going to bed by ten, which he loved, so this wasn't typical. "Are you sure you're okay?" he asked, slightly suspicious. He was probably thinking the same thing I was about possible mania, but I didn't say anything because I was feeling too good and didn't want him to ruin it.

"The doctor says this will change once I get accustomed to the new medications," I lied, downplaying his concerns. "I feel fine, though." David nodded warily at my explanation and asked me to be careful. The truth was, I wasn't my usual self and didn't care why. I woke up refreshed after just three or four hours of sleep, and my body hummed like a well-oiled machine throughout the day. My creative energy was crackling on high and the focus was the job. In addition to my human resources and volunteer duties, Ted had asked me to oversee the food bank because of my experience there. Building the human resources department, hiring and training new staff, and having a hand in the food bank meant my days were jammed full of meetings, interviews, and paperwork. I loved it.

* * *

It was 4:00 a.m. I was wide awake and driving around in my car as I had been doing secretly for the past few weeks. My skyrocketing success at work had fueled an obsession with the place. To avoid conflict with David, I would go to bed when he did, lay there waiting for him to fall asleep, and then sneak out of the house. I'd drive by the food bank and imagine how the front entrance could be re-engineered for rain cover and disability access, then go home and sketch out designs. Ted had me involved in the inner workings of his plan to reorganize management staff, which meant promotions and new hiring. It also meant layoffs, which had to be meticulously executed to avoid lawsuits. This was the big league of human resources and I relished the challenge of it. I also worried about what terminating staff members would do to their lives, but hoped I might be able to do something to lessen the blow.

I had a meeting scheduled with Ted at 7:00 a.m. to review staff layoffs, and suddenly I felt compelled to make a beeline to the office to make sure I would be ready. That would give me three hours to prepare. On the way there, my head exploded with run-together thoughts that ran counter to my self-confidence. Suddenly I felt overwhelmed by the multitude of things we needed to discuss and all that I needed to prepare up front so I wouldn't forget later, and what if Ted asked me questions I didn't know the answers to, and how could I possibly keep up with all these projects, and why should he be firing people, and should I do anything to stop it? Was there anything I could even do? The necessity to sideline Ted's plan was drilling a hole into my brain. Then it hit me: I could destroy the employee files.

My body was trembling by the time I came to a stop in front of the office. My heart was thumping in my chest as I walked up the concrete steps to the front door. Where was my key? I searched my pockets frantically but found nothing. I grabbed the handle and rattled the glass door, hoping to dislodge it from the latch. It didn't budge. But this couldn't wait. I had to save those employees. The clock was ticking and I grew panicky that Ted would arrive before I was ready. Seized by urgency, I crashed my foot through the plate glass door as adrenaline surged through my veins. A jumble of thoughts ricocheted in my head. It was outrageous what Ted was doing and I had to stop him. He was going to ruin people's lives. But wait, look at me and my superhuman strength: I could walk through locked doors! I stormed into Ted's office and swept everything off his desk, including the computer monitor, which went crashing to the floor. I opened the file cabinets of employee records and pulled out every folder, tossing them into the air. The evidence, I had to get rid of it. I pulled over a bookcase and watched more files and papers fall to the floor. Sweating profusely and gasping for breath, I fell to the ground and urinated myself. Sprawled out flat on my back and staring at the ceiling, I thought: What have I just done?

What could have been hours later but felt like minutes, I heard a car door slam out front and knew that Ted had arrived. It must be 7 a.m. My body began to shake as my mental chaos roiled. What was he going to say when he saw me? How was I going to explain what had happened? And why did I just wreck his office? The front door opened and I heard shards of glass fall to the ground. My trembling turned into gushing sobs as soon as Ted's face came into view at his office door.

"What the hell is going on, Steve?" His tone was sharp; he clearly disapproved. My sobbing cries turned into wailing gibberish as I spit out an incoherent string of words describing what had happened. As I babbled on, Ted's eyes turned to my urine-soaked jeans. That's when his face softened. He reached out his hand to help me stand and guided me to sit down in his chair. "I can help you through this. Just try to relax and catch your breath." I trusted this man completely. He had me sitting in the executive director's chair; maybe this was his way of saying he was going to promote me again. He must have recognized that my intuition to save the employees was the right thing to do. I loved this guy! Everything was going to be all right.

And that's when I heard the sirens and saw the red lights flashing outside the window. Why were the police here? Suddenly, the room was filled with men in uniform wearing guns and shouting at me to stand up and put my hands behind my head. I was paralyzed and couldn't move. Ted was saying something to the officers about an obvious mental break and that I was a trusted staff person who was sick.

They weren't buying it and reached over to grab my arm when Ted stepped in front of me and snapped sternly, "I *said* he is a trusted staff person and I will take responsibility to see that he cooperates." The police backed down and the paramedics were ushered in. Wow, Ted really did recognize what I was trying to do! When he guided me from his chair to the gurney, I felt like a prince. As I was whisked out of the office and through the smashed door, my body was calm. Ted must have arranged for me to go to a special place to rest. Everyone was so nice and talked to me kindly. When the gurney was lifted into the back of the ambulance and a cute paramedic leaned in close to get my pulse, I wanted to kiss him. Instead, I spit in his face. Then people weren't so nice. Two of them came out of nowhere and held me down while someone out of sight pulled a netted hood tightly over my head. My hands and feet were tied down and I was completely immobilized. Voices were screaming in my head. What just happened? Why did I do that? As I looked out through the small holes of the netted shroud, another voice took over: Wow, this was a pretty efficient way to keep me from spitting on them. Clever, those paramedics.

* * *

Once I got through the obligatory process: hospital, psych ward, and an extended work leave for recuperation, things gradually returned to normal at home. David was relieved that the whole thing was over. He didn't chase after me as he had done with the prior manic episode; he said he just didn't have the energy for it. He was glad I was better, and I was happy to have my anchor back.

Work wasn't going as smoothly, though. While Ted was saying all the right things, I could sense his wariness. To my questions he would respond matter-of-factly with none of the personal affect we'd shared before. Passing in the parking lot, he would avoid eye contact. I was walking on eggshells and was scared I might lose my job. I had lost his trust and was desperate to regain it. From my human resources training, I knew I was being carefully managed, so I decided to get my doctor on a three-way call in hopes of relieving Ted's suspicions.

Dr. Peterson was immediately apologetic. "He is a new patient of mine and his allergy to the drug I prescribed was clearly in his chart; I just missed it." I felt horrible. My face flushed with shame as I listened to him take the blame for my inaction. I knew I hadn't revealed to him my history with Prednisone and I wanted to slap myself for withholding that from him.

But while the call from the doctor supported my case, Ted remained wary. He kept our meetings formal and brief and I could feel the scrutiny, as if I were being viewed through a microscope. As I realized the only way to regain his trust would be to demonstrate what I was capable of, I devised a twofold plan that I hoped would do the trick. One, arrive at the office early to get a jump on the day and make sure Ted knew I was working and available. And two, focus on acquainting myself with the hundred or so staff members at six different locations around the city to gain wide employee support. On top of my regular duties, I spent additional hours in the field traveling from thrift store to thrift store, meeting with employees and learning how they did their jobs. I was spending fifty to sixty hours each week keeping my head down and focused on proving to Ted that I deserved to be back in his good graces. Despite my best attempts, though, the ice between us did not melt. After three months of nonstop trying, I was ready to call it quits.

"Should I just look for another job?" I spilled out as David and I had our evening chat. "I'm busting my ass and he barely notices. Sometimes it feels as though he doesn't want me there anymore." It was stressing me out not knowing if I was going to get past this, and hanging in limbo was driving me nuts.

"You know that's not true," he shot back. "You're the best thing that's happened to the place and Ted knows it." If he does, he's not showing it, I mumbled to myself. "He just needs to be sure you're fully recovered," David finished. As I absorbed these words, I surmised that he was right. Ted was a fair man and I just needed to give him more time. I decided to hunker down and stick it out for the long haul.

Sometime later, I was heading to the office when a call came from Malorie, the thrift store manager in Renton. The minute I answered, she started talking. "We've been robbed," she told me, and went on about how she found the place when she arrived. The bay window had been smashed, cash register torn off the counter, and the safe was missing from her office. "The police are on their way," she finished.

"So am I," I said as we hung up. When I arrived, Malorie introduced me to the police officer, who gave me a brief report on their findings. The safe was recovered in a nearby alley, busted open and emptied. A report would be filed, but there was little chance that the culprits would be found. When the officer left, Malorie and I talked about what was needed to secure the place.

"It's going to cost thousands to repair everything," Malorie noted. "It pisses me off when this happens, and it's especially galling that we have to spend that kind of money on something other than the people who need it." Malorie was still chewing on this, clearly agitated by the injustice caused to the people we served. Suddenly, her face lit up. "We should call TV stations and tell them what happened. Maybe we could get something on the news and drum up some sympathy donations." It was genius. I had our marketing department contact the local news channels. Incredibly, they bit into the story and a reporter was on the way. It had all moved fast, so when I asked Malorie if she was ready to be on the news, her face froze. "There's no way I'm going on camera; I'd babble like an idiot. You have to do it." Stage fright was

FEARFULLY, WONDERFULLY MADE

never a problem for me, so I quickly pulled together some thoughts and when the reporter arrived with a camera person in tow, I was able to answer her questions about what had happened. Asked if I had any last thoughts, I made a direct appeal to listeners. "Whoever robbed this store was taking money that helped feed and house families. Donations would help us defray the cost of repairs and would be greatly appreciated."

The story aired that night, and as David watched it, he kept looking over at me, smiling. "You did a great job. If Ted doesn't say something about this, he's a moron and doesn't deserve you." I hoped he was right. As if overhearing our conversation, I got a text message from Ted that said "Nice job on the news. Let's talk in the morning." My skin tingled as I read his words. I held up the phone for David to read.

"See, I told you." I struggled not to obsess about what Ted might say in the morning, but felt hopeful that the thawing had begun between us.

"I've been getting calls from businesses around the Renton store," Ted started, the minute I walked into his office, waving me to sit down. "All of them offered to donate goods and services to help us repair the damage and make the store more secure. Nice work." I lit up from head to toe as he continued with the details of the calls. He was obviously pleased; his tone and demeanor had nearly returned to the way it used to be.

"There's something else I want to talk about," Ted said as he glanced my way with a serious look on his face. Uh-oh. Here it comes. The months of arctic relations were coming to a head and it could go either way. His eyes were fixed on mine as he went on.

"Just because I haven't said anything doesn't mean I haven't noticed how hard you've been working, but I needed to be certain you were better. I am now." The air was motionless in anticipation, but after living in fear of losing my job, I could feel myself breathe again. Something had clicked back into place, like a switch flipping things back to normal. We spent the next few minutes talking more about the incident at the Renton store and how the donations were pouring in. Then I updated him on a few other things that were happening, just like we used to. As I was getting ready to leave, Ted said nonchalantly, "Oh, by the way, I want to promote you to the Director of Human Resources. Congratulations."

22

The Start of Something Sinister. 2011

I soaked up the cool morning air as sunlight shimmered off the waves rolling on the lake. Old growth douglas fir and western red cedar trees soared into the sky mottling the asphalt path before us in swaying shadows. We were at Seward Park, strolling on a pathway that encircles a 300-acre forest. Lost in our individual thoughts, David abruptly broke the silence. "I've always loved walking around Green Lake," he said, with all the certainty of someone who had lived in Seattle his entire life. I waited for him to catch his error, but he said nothing.

"You mean Seward Park," I nudged. He stopped and looked at the lake, then back to the path. He turned to me, his face painted with bewilderment. I had an urge to shake him—How could he not recognize where we were? He should have known this wasn't Green Lake—Hell, he grew up in that neighborhood. Green Lake was nestled into a tidy neighborhood of homes and businesses, whereas Seward Park was a forest jutting into a large bay that is part of the much larger Lake Washington; there was no confusing the two. This was baffling and my mind began to spin as I started to imagine the implications. Was this a sign of Alzheimer's? God, please no!

"Are you sure?" he questioned warily, while continuing to survey the surroundings. The look of utter bafflement on his face sent a chill up my spine. I'd been trying to ignore the warning signs that had started a couple years ago—like forgetting names of people he had known all his life—but it had become increasingly noticeable in the last twelve months. It was especially apparent during our evening conversations. I noticed the volume of his voice was lower and he'd forget something that was just said to him. He was unable to follow the thread of our conversations and was constantly asking me to repeat myself. We would joke about his advancing age and laugh it off, but this new development put a new level of terror in me because I feared what was coming.

David's dad had exhibited similar symptoms at the start of his Alzheimer's a decade ago. For a while, David's mom had downplayed her husband's steady decline, but we knew something wasn't right. His dad was more subdued in conversations, not talking with his usual gusto, and sometimes said little. "He's just tired," David's mom would say, trying to cover it up. Her husband didn't want anyone to know, so she dutifully complied. That all changed one night when she called us, frantic, at 3 a.m.

"Your father is in the garage cleaning guns and I'm scared he's going to get hurt and he's not listening to me," she blurted out in an avalanche of words I could hear through the phone at David's ear. We jumped into the car and drove over; David's hands gripped the steering wheel as we tried to keep ourselves from imagining what we might find. Would his dad be confrontational? Accidentally shoot himself? What about his mom? Was she safe?

When we arrived, his dad was no longer in the garage and was not pleased to see us at his front door. David right away started asking questions about the guns but was cut off before he got any answers.

"I'm a grown man and know what I'm doing," his dad fumed, clearly agitated by the encounter. "Your mother worries too much."

After the incident, we paid much closer attention to his parents. David was especially worried about his mom and insisted she get some help. When we arranged for a cleaning service, though, they were abruptly turned away when David's dad answered the door in hot protest.

"We don't need any help," he thundered, slamming the door. When he was eventually diagnosed with Alzheimer's, the word struck fear in David—he knew this was often handed down. He preferred not to speak about it because he wasn't ready to face it, so we swept it to the side and pretended everything was fine.

As David and I continued to walk around Seward Park, my thoughts jumped to work. Because I was the human resources director, David was required to copy me on certain emails he sent to staff, and I had begun to notice a decline in his communication skills. When I brought it up to him, pointing out missing punctuation and nonsensical words, he didn't respond right away.

"I don't know what happened," he finally said, and the look on his face gave away his obvious frustration. We both knew what this meant—that what was happening at home was now affecting his work, something neither of us wanted to admit. Instead, David deflected. "I guess it's just old age." I was at a loss as to how to respond. Because his job meant everything to him, he was clearly not ready to admit defeat. And my persisting would create awkwardness at home. His punctuation and grammar errors weren't doing any damage, I rationalized, so I left it alone.

What I couldn't leave alone, though, was how frighteningly similar David was now to when his dad had started his decline. Once Alzheimer's took hold of him, it wasn't long before he was moved into an assisted-living facility. Would I have to do the same thing with David? Would he get as ill as his dad, who was eventually diapered and fed with a spoon? Next, my thoughts leapt to his mom and what it must have been like for her behind closed doors. She had become the housemaid for her husband who had regressed to a belligerent infant—a faint reflection of the capable man she had married. My body shivered when it hit me: maybe this was my future and it had already begun.

I waited until we were home from Seward Park before I mentioned his confusion. After a few minutes of discussion, David agreed it was time to get his memory checked.

"We still don't know anything for sure," he stressed, "but if it *is* Alzheimer's, I'd rather know that now. I don't want to replicate my dad's situation and put you through what my mom experienced." He reached over and stroked my arm. My chest swelled with love and sorrow. David's life was in peril, and yet he was concerned about me. I held back my rising tears as the moment passed.

Several weeks later, we forced ourselves through the familiar doors of the medical building where our appointment with the neurologist was scheduled. It was the same location where we had met with the surgeon who had removed David's brain tumor just seven years earlier. A familiar twinge of fear began to build. Would we learn of something equally as horrible that was going on inside David's brain? I stuffed that thought down deep as we entered the building. "Here we go again," David said, smiling meekly. I wondered what he was thinking. All I could see in my mind's eye were the staples in his forehead.

Half an hour later, we were seated with the doctor in his office, David with a clipboard and me throwing up silent prayers to the heavens. The doctor was explaining the instructions. "Before I start asking you simple questions, I want you to remember the word 'dog,' and keep that word in your memory until I ask you for it." David's face crinkled into concentration, as if what the doctor had described was a calculus problem. Once the test began, I stayed as quiet as a mouse would be if a big black cat was stalking nearby. My nerves were on edge as I watched David work hard to answer the simplest of questions. He managed to get through them when the doctor asked him to repeat the word from earlier. I was straining to send telepathic messages to him: *Say Dog, Damn it, Dog!* David made some guesses but could not recall the word. I slumped inside. This was the same man who could pull Latin phrases out of thin air in front of hundreds of parishioners, the same man who could speak with such flowing eloquence that people would dissolve into tears— and now he could barely remember the simplest things. This was the cruelest trick the Universe could play on him.

The doctor then repeated the test with a new word to remember, followed by some easy questions. When he asked David to repeat the word, he failed again. I could sense the growing alarm in the room. As this went on for the next twenty minutes, all I could think about was how similar he sounded to our declining evening conversations. He just wasn't able to keep track of what was being said, and this test was showing that in spades. I felt a hole form in my stomach. The reality washed over me—there could be no more relegating this to normal old-age forgetfulness.

The doctor finished up the test. David had not been able to repeat any of the words he was asked to remember. The defeat and frustration on his face was palpable. I grabbed his hand to let him know I understood how he felt. He smiled faintly as the doctor began speaking. "You definitely have signs of memory loss. It is unusual for someone so young, but the test clearly shows a problem with short-term memory." Memory loss? That was a terribly vague term. I was fuming as I stared at him—what a lame-ass thing to say. Was the doctor worried about depressing David? Why was he trying to sugar-coat this? I got it, it was hard news to deliver, but he was doing us no favor by keeping us in the dark.

"Is it Alzheimer's, Doctor?" I pressed. He shifted uncomfortably in his chair. David's eyes were glued to his face, waiting for an answer to the question he was afraid to ask. My heart was in my throat, aware that our shelter of not knowing was about to come crashing down. As much as I wanted an answer, nothing would be the same once we knew the truth. How would this change the sweet life that David and I had finally arrived at? How fast would it come on? How would it change our relationship? Would this be how David died? My heart was racing as the doctor answered my question.

"This test is only one of the diagnostic tools we have for Alzheimer's, but given the family history, it's likely what you have." A silent bomb detonated in my head, his words delivering a sweeping blow to the middle of my chest. Even though I had expected it, hearing the doctor say the word made my world explode. We had just gotten back on our feet after years of hanging in limbo and this is what awaits us? I was barely listening as the doctor kept talking. "We can perform an MRI or a spinal fluid test to be more conclusive, but you were right to come in. It's always better to catch this sooner rather than later." Wait, what was he saying? Did it really make that much difference by catching it sooner? A flicker of hope lit up the dark cloud in my head.

I looked at the doctor expectantly. "Is there anything we can do to treat it?"

For a brief moment, it looked like he wanted to take back what he said. "There is no cure but there is a medication that has shown promise in slowing down the progression," he replied. "We can get him started on that right away." I looked at David, searching his face for a clue to his feelings while trying to hide my own. What I saw shocked me: his frustration had melted into acceptance. I had seen this expression on him before—when he let go of the priesthood after his brain surgery. That was all well and good for him, but what about me? I was going to be the one dealing with David all the time. His mom was watching his dad every second of every day. Her husband's explosions and insults had beaten her down. He couldn't even remember her name. She had to drop everything—but at least she was retired. I had finally gotten back on track at work—how was I going to watch over him? Would this be the end of my short career? And then I thought—who cares about the job? This was my David. I couldn't bear the thought of losing him so soon. He was only sixty-seven. My mind was reeling, trying to make sense of this massive injustice. I needed to get a grip. Forcing myself to rationalize a hopeful outcome, my thoughts churned:

The doctor said there were medications that might slow it down.

He said he could perform more conclusive tests.

David's dad was well into his eighties before he needed help.

We got on this early so there's still a chance for things to get better.

Scientists will come up with something.

He still has plenty of time.

23

Hawaii Brings A Glimpse of the Future. 2012

The peace that permeated the household rippled softly through my body as I leaned back into the overstuffed chair savoring my morning coffee. It had been nearly a year since the diagnosis, and things had gone surprisingly well. Within a month of getting the news from the doctor, David retired from his job and assumed the role of homemaker, something that had mostly been my job before I was working. He kept our home picked up, did the laundry, walked Jetta, and had dinner on the table every night when I got home from work. It was as if the natural order of things had been restored—the elder was retired instead of the younger one.

As I watched David in the kitchen, a startling thought took over my mind: David had gotten old on me. When we first met, I didn't notice the nineteen-year age difference. David was youthful, jogged several miles a day, and had such vitality and vigor that we felt close in age. Even now at sixty-eight, he had a full head of curly brown hair with not a gray one to be found. But he also had an incurable disease that would rob him of his memory and eventually take his life. And unlike for AIDS, there was no treatment. There was no time to waste.

"Hey, remember what you promised me when I turned fifty?" I stated as David joined me for coffee.

"I sure do. We're going to Hawaii!" he replied enthusiastically. Reaching fifty had been a pipe dream when I was twenty-nine and there was no treatment for AIDS. But when I was thirty-five and the new drugs suddenly made it possible, we made a pact—a trip to Hawaii to celebrate when I turned fifty. I got busy booking the flight and picking out the luxury suite that would mark this special milestone. Now all we needed to do was wait for the travel date to arrive.

All was well on the flight, but as soon as we checked in and got to our suite, David became agitated. Instead of noticing the magnificent room with the large balcony and sweeping views of the ocean, he became consumed with unpacking his luggage and finding places to put his things. Watching his obvious frustration as he tried to get organized shocked me. He was never like this. "Are you okay?" I nudged. When he didn't reply, a blanket of fear settled over me. I recalled a conversation with the neurologist about David having early-onset Alzheimer's, which advances more rapidly. Was it taking hold already? I headed out to the balcony to scour the internet for an answer while he rummaged through his luggage. I ran across an article on the Alzheimer's Association website that mentioned how the stress of a new location can bring on this kind of behavior—that it can seriously affect their sense of order. That certainly explained things. I thought getting him out of the hotel room might help.

"Do you feel like taking a walk to explore what's around us?" I asked him when I came inside. He had finished unpacking, although things weren't as tidy as he used to make them whenever we'd travel.

"Okay, I think I'm done here," he replied. I ignored the mess of his clothes piled on the bed and pulled him outside.

The sun streaked through the sky heading steadily toward the horizon. We took off our sandals and sunk our feet into the warm sand. Walking hand in hand along the ocean's edge sent warm feelings coursing through me, the comfort of his touch that comes with twenty years of togetherness. Maybe his muddled mind would straighten itself out.

I spotted an amazing restaurant with dining right on the sandy beach. "How about there for dinner?" I said, pointing at the spot for David.

"Perfect," he replied.

"Should we order something special for the occasion?" I asked David once we were seated. He nodded yes but did so while he looked out at the ocean and didn't offer a suggestion. Instead of pressing it, I just ordered for both of us. Once the waiter had poured the champagne, we clinked our glasses together and savored the moment as David looked absently back at the ocean. I was all grins, but David was clearly distracted and didn't make the kind of fuss I was expecting. Despite my sinking feeling, I picked out the richest menu item they offered: lobster poached in butter with wine sauce. As we ate in silence, I began to wonder whether David knew why we were eating such an elaborate meal. I looked around at the other couples, animated in their conversation and interpersonal body language. Watching them—seeing their connection, their happiness—launched a raft of longing that I realized would no longer be satisfied by the man sitting beside me.

Instead of sulking, I decided to jog his memory. "You seem more relaxed than before," I started, trying to get the conversation going. "Are you feeling better?"

He nodded, "Yes, I don't know why I was so flustered before; I just felt so out of sorts." I reached over, squeezing his hand.

"I've been reading it's pretty common with Alzheimer's to get disoriented in new surroundings, so that must be why you were confused." David nodded, glad for the reassurance. "Do you remember the main reason we came to Hawaii?" I decided to just tell him when his face drew a blank at my question—I didn't want to be hard on him. "It's my fiftieth birthday and we came here to celebrate my survival. You know, the one you predicted."

He looked at me keenly while searching his memory. "That's right. I totally forgot about it." He reached across the table and took both my hands. "I'm really sorry." His gentle voice cracked me wide open. It was all I could do to hold back the tears.

Later that night, after David had gone to bed and I was still too wound up to sleep, I went out on the veranda and gazed at the blackness of the ocean stretching out before me. It was a moonless night, the only light coming from a passing ship. As much as I tried to push it back, I couldn't shake how badly the day had gone. David was losing it, fast, and it was all I could do to keep myself from crumbling into a massive heap of despair. Even though David now knew why we were here, it was clear he could not grasp the significance of it. The decades of closeness we had shared were turning into a fossilized memory for him, a memory I would now have to carry on alone. We had survived so much over the years, but this brain disorder would wipe out his recollection of our life together. It was heartbreaking to realize he would forget everything about us.

And then a thought crossed my mind that grabbed hold of me so fiercely I nearly cried out in agony: I was losing my second partner. Twenty-two years earlier, I was reeling from the same excruciating truth after Tom was suddenly gone, and here it was, starting to happen all over again. Only this time, David was still here, and he was leaving me slowly. I wasn't sure which was worse. It was impossible to shake the feelings of loneliness and grief that saturated my body.

The next morning, things felt lighter. David seemed more settled; he was reading the newspaper and drinking coffee when I padded into the living room. After kissing him good morning, I walked out onto the patio deck and breathed in the salty ocean air. We were in Hawaii! There was no reason to ruin a perfectly good vacation feeling sorry for myself. I certainly knew what we liked to do on vacations, so I set aside my hopeless mood from the previous night and decided to make the most of our time there.

"Let's go see the sights," I suggested. "We can drive by the lava fields and take a walk through the tropical park." As we drove around the lush landscape of the island, the climate in the car was subdued. There was a comfort to our closeness as we held hands, but something was off again.

"I've never seen a black sandy beach before, have you?" I asked David as he stared out the window.

"I don't think so," he replied quietly. I expected him to say more, to express some awe at the sight, but it never came. We pulled off the road to take a picture of a huge leafy plant and as David posed in front of it to illustrate the size—which towered over his head—he stood there with an expressionless gaze. It was painfully obvious that he was standing there only because I asked him to, not because he was fascinated with the sight. Pulling back onto the highway, I swallowed my disappointment and decided to try something that might get a reaction.

"How about we go get a drink and watch the naked dancers at the strip club?" This was something he always loved to do, and he was still definitely game.

David's eyes practically popped out of his head as he took in the twisting bodies of the young men. It wasn't Provincetown—we weren't dancing and picking up guys—but it was keeping our mood elevated and the elephant out of the room for a while. We spent the week driving along the coastline, eating Hawaiian food, and soaking in the laid-back vibe of the island. Thankfully, David's long-term memories were still intact so he could reminisce with me about the dozens of places we had been together. It felt like old times, and yet I feared the reprieve was only temporary. Unfortunately, my instinct turned out to be right; the undoing started the morning of our departure.

The sudden disruption in our leisurely routine wreaked havoc on David's calmed state. I had taken care of the packing and getting us to the airport, but he was confused and grumpy, not understanding why we had to leave. The airport was crowded, and as we dragged our bags to the ticket counter, David stopped dead in his tracks ... "How do you know where we're going?" he asked, exasperated. "I don't have my tickets and ...."

183

"We're going to miss our plane if you just stand there," I snapped, cutting him off. The usual stress of travel was amplified by his lack of cooperation. "Now come on and follow me; I know where we're going." He picked up the sharp tone in my voice and did what I said. David was still agitated when we got to the counter to obtain our boarding passes and check our bags, but at least he was quiet. As we made our way through the crowded terminal to our gate, it was all I could do to keep my eye on David while also figuring out where we were headed. Confused, he stopped again, dropping his bag.

"Are you sure you're going in the right direction," he cried out, "Where are you taking me?" I tried to keep my cool by explaining it in simple terms.

"Look," I said, pointing at the boarding pass, "It says gate G8. We're at G5 now so we're getting close." He stared at the pass, then looked up at the gate number. "Come on, let's go or we're going to miss our flight." He picked up his bag and kept following me.

By the time we got to our seats, I was sweaty and exhausted. All I wanted was to chug down a handful of the single-shooter liquor bottles. David, on the other hand, seemed unfazed and quickly fell fast asleep. Watching him, I wondered if he would even remember this vacation. Would he completely forget the reason we went all that way? Instead of celebrating this monumental birthday we had both wished for, this trip would be forever etched in my mind as the time I realized my David was slipping away from me.

As the plane landed in Seattle, gray clouds and rainy skies covered the horizon, illuminating the gloominess of what was yet to come.

24

The Unraveling Begins. 2012

When we were in public, David appeared normal. He looked the same. He nodded and smiled at all the right times. But at home, it was an entirely different story. Arriving from work each evening, invigorated from the day and eager to tell him all about it, I'd find him either asleep or staring at the television. There was no dinner ready and the house was a mess. Even in Hawaii, he was at least asking some questions and able to reminisce, but now there were times when he barely spoke at all. When I asked him what he did that day, he'd often mumble something about walking Jetta and then fall silent. It was so hard to reconcile this with the David I knew before—the David who *lived* to preach and loved to converse. But now, he could hardly string a sentence together. Feeling both lonely and suffocated in his presence was a crushing development. Mornings were a little better—he was more alert and in a happier mood—but there still wasn't much to talk about and I'd rush off to work. Truth was, I preferred to be there most of the time and looked forward to leaving the house each day. As much as I hated to admit it, work was a lot more stimulating and I spent more and more time there. At least there I was having conversations, learning new things, and getting a lot done. This was a heart-wrenching change in our relationship and it made me numb inside when I let myself imagine where it was going.

One night, about three months after our Hawaii trip, I was getting ready for bed when David came out of his bedroom and grabbed his coat. We were sleeping in separate rooms at night because of his erratic nighttime patterns.

"Where are you going?" I asked. It was after midnight and he'd been asleep since seven. I noticed he was getting Jetta trussed up for a walk.

He looked at me and wrinkled his brow in annoyance. "Where does it look like?" He was headed for the door when I pressed further.

"But it's dark out and time for bed." I tried to stay calm. I remembered how it used to be me sneaking out at night. David's face drew a blank look.

"No, it's not. I just woke up. It's morning." My gut tightened. I had read about this. It was Sundown Syndrome, so called because it takes effect after the sun sets, which can cause restlessness, disorientation, pacing, and yelling. I was seeing it in David now.

"Come over here and look out the window," I said as he followed me into the living room. "See, the streetlights are on and the sky is dark." It was obvious from his expression that he wasn't following my logic. This was a new level of confusion for him. He looked outside but said nothing, then turned around and went for the door with Jetta in tow.

"Whatever time it is, I'm still going out," David nearly shouted. I decided not to push it and grabbed my coat, following him out the door. I knew I had to go with him because the last few weeks had become increasingly harrowing. It had started with his erratic driving. After he had nearly run over a pedestrian, I had convinced him to give up driving and take the bus. That worked for a while, until he started falling asleep and missing his stop, getting off at the wrong place miles away. When he would call me, lost, it was hard to get a straight answer as to where he was. Fortunately, I could track his phone location and go pick him up. But that only solved one of the problems. Just a few days earlier, Jetta had been attacked by another dog while David was walking her. When it lunged for Jetta, David kicked it away, but the dog went back for her and punctured her skin as it clamped onto her neck. The dog took off after another kick, but it scared me to think what else might happen.

A few nights later, I was awakened by the ringing of the telephone. "Why isn't the food bank open?" David asked urgently as soon as I answered. He had been volunteering there since retiring from St. Vincent de Paul, but it was 11:00 p.m. Why was he calling me? He must have gotten out of bed.

"Where are you?" I asked, a gnawing worry crawling across my skin.

"I'm at the food bank," he replied. "It opens at eleven, so why is no one here?" He sounded panicky. I was already pulling on clothes and heading for the car.

"You just got the times mixed up, that's all," I tried to reassure him. "Stay where you are and I'll be there in a flash." I fought back panic and frustration as I drove the ten minutes to his location. How did he get out of the house without me knowing? It was dark outside—he had clearly lost the ability to tell the difference between night and day. The food bank isn't in the best neighborhood—what if someone robs him, or worse? I drove as fast as I could without breaking the speed limit. Relief washed over me when I arrived—he was there—but it quickly turned to anguish when I watched him closely. His shoulders were slouched, and he appeared lost, staring off into the distance. He looked as though he had aged twenty years in the year since his diagnosis. I wanted to cry. How could this be happening so fast?

What was he thinking about as he stood on the empty porch? Was he even aware of how bad his mind was getting? And what about us? Heat rose in my chest and flushed my scalp with sweat, anxiety taking hold of me. I had spent the past months telling myself that this was just the natural order of things—that no one gets off this planet alive. It all sounded good, but it was just theoretical, feel-good drivel. How can this be happening? I was boiling with a helpless rage that had nowhere to go and no one to blame.

David finally noticed me and descended the steps to the car. I composed myself before he opened the door.

"Are you okay?" I concentrated on keeping my voice calm.

"Yes, but I don't know what I was thinking. I guess I got mixed up, like you said." There wasn't much more to say, but I was already planning how to better keep track of him. A front door alarm would be installed, and I would also insist David wear a secondary tracking device in the form of a bracelet. It was obvious I couldn't leave him at home alone anymore. Aside from the problem of him leaving in the night, he was either getting routinely lost when he walked Jetta or was sleeping all day. I connected with a local senior care agency, and they sent over visitors while I was at work during the day, but this only lasted a couple of weeks. "I don't know these people and I don't want them here," he bemoaned after one volunteer rubbed him the wrong way. Just like his dad, I thought. The next thing I tried was dropping him off at senior daycare programs while I was at work. He liked this for a while, and then suddenly he didn't. I was in the middle of a meeting when a call from the senior care facility interrupted my presentation.

"Mr. Knipp, this is Sonya from the center. David just left the building and is walking down the street." What? my head screamed. "Don't worry, though," she went on quickly, "he's fine. We have two orderlies following him, but please come to get him." Damn it! I didn't have time for this.

"Okay, I'm on my way," I replied, trying to hide my frustration. I hung up the phone, excused myself from the meeting, and got into the car. Now what? What was I going to do with him? It was the middle of the workday and there was no one I could call. His friends had stopped offering to help, and it was not like they could manage him anyway. The only option was to take him with me back to the office.

When I pulled up alongside the curb where David was walking—with two orderlies dressed in white trailing a few feet behind him—I noticed the irritated look on his face. He launched into a tirade the second he was in the car.

"There's nothing but old people there, and none of them say anything, and I don't like playing stupid games, and I'd rather be home with Jetta, and I don't ever want to go back." He finished his rant by folding his arms and turning towards the window. I gauged my words carefully because I didn't want to set him off and make the rest of the day even worse.

"You don't have to go back. We can find something else for you to do," I said, although I had no idea what that might be. Instead of trying to figure it out then, I took him back to the office with me and decided to talk about it later. Trying to keep him seated while I worked at my desk proved next to impossible. He was like a six-year-old boy in the body of a sixty-eight-year-old man: cranky, persistent, and vocal. He wouldn't sit still, and it wasn't like I could lock him in a closet, even though I wanted to. I felt terrible, but I had no idea how to handle him in this state.

"You can't hold me here," he barked when I closed my office door to keep him from roaming the halls. "Jetta needs a walk and I want to go home." His voice was loud. He was mad and was being unreasonable. I didn't know what to do, so resorted to a fib.

"If you don't sit down, I'm going to lose my job," I said, trying to plead with something he understood. His parents had instilled a very strong work ethic in him and I hoped it would give him pause. "You don't want that to happen, do you?" I thought that guilt would do the trick and it worked. He finally quieted down, eventually dozing off until it was time to go home.

The next day, Ted popped into my office. "Hey, what happened yesterday?" I could see both the curiosity and concern on his face.

"Yeah, sorry about that. David left the adult day care center and I had nowhere to take him but here." With any other boss I would have been more tentative about bringing it up, but Ted had been so supportive of both of us and I knew I was in a safe space.

He took a minute to respond. I could tell he was interested in solving the problem.

"I understand. Tell you what, why don't you work from home until things get sorted with David. Take as much time as you need." I knew he was trying to help, but he didn't realize that work had become my last remaining refuge. There was nothing else I could do, though. I was grateful to Ted, but sick about what this meant for me; I would be with David day and night, and I wasn't sure I could survive without a break from him. The heaviness of this landed like a boulder in my gut. How could it get any worse?

25

Collapse. 2012

I stared at the words on the check David had written, trying to hold it together. I looked at the payee line again, struggling to make sense of it: *To the Magnificent Mother Theresa, whom I love and adore.* It was written for five-thousand dollars. Really? Mother Theresa? Wasn't she dead already? What on earth was he thinking? If this check ever got sent, would it even be cashed? Would someone take one look at this and realize the person who wrote it could be scammed? It was still sitting in his checkbook, signed but not removed from the pack. I tore it from the checkbook and ripped it up, certain he had already forgotten about it. Still, I needed to do something I wanted to avoid—ask his doctor to declare him incompetent. Having his power of attorney, it was my responsibility to keep his assets safe. Friends had already reported seeing him give fifty-dollar bills to homeless people, and I started seeing late notices and payment reminders in the mail. The only way to protect his money was to legally remove his access to the account. It was daunting to take over his finances and the last thing I wanted to do. At least that's what I thought.

When I arrived back at our apartment several hours later, after returning from a walk, I nearly choked on the smell of excrement. "David, do you smell that?" I shouted as I walked into the living room, thinking Jetta must have had an accident. When he didn't appear, I headed into his bedroom, where the smell got stronger. I found him standing in the adjoining bathroom. He was in front of the toilet, pants down to his ankles, a trail of diarrhea running down his leg and into his shoes. The toilet seat was smeared with it. He was standing there with his hands covered in it, not sure what to do. My mind was reeling; how was I supposed to deal with this? I wanted to turn and run away. Despite my churning stomach, duty kicked in. I took a deep breath through my mouth and stepped inside.

"Let's get your clothes off," I managed, moving close to him so he could use me for balance. I tried not to flinch as he placed his shit-covered hands on my shoulder. He kicked his shoes off first; then we got his socks, pants, and underwear off. Now it was all over my hands and it took every ounce of my strength not to freak out. "Take your shirt off and we'll get you into the shower," I said. I got the water running. After David got in, I picked up the soiled clothes and cleaned up the mess, then fled to the other shower to clean myself up. As the water ran over me, I let my tears of despair flow.

Was it just an accident? I couldn't get much out of David when I asked him. He was embarrassed by the whole thing and had little to say. I was totally grossed out and hoped it was just a one-time thing, but over the next few weeks his toilet hygiene steadily declined. While no more explosive scenes happened, he wasn't wiping himself carefully and had shit-stained underwear. He wasn't keen for me to help him, so I bit my lip and tried to respect his privacy. This became next to impossible, though, as the house began to smell like a latrine. Sometimes the mess soaked through his pants and got on the furniture; it was getting to be too much. I wanted to help him, but I wasn't sure how much longer I could do this.

The final straw came with the familiar sound of the door alarm several weeks later—it meant he had left the apartment. It had become a stress trigger for me and its particular tone bolted me out of bed. I grabbed my robe and when I opened the door to go after him, David turned around and made a beeline toward me. "I want to go out for breakfast," he practically yelled. "I'm hungry." Although it was after midnight, he must have thought it was morning.

"What's going on?"

"I said I'm hungry and want to go have breakfast." His words were not a request but a demand from a man who was towering over me. The hair on my neck stood up. "It's after midnight, David," I replied, trying not to show my growing irritation. "I have to work in the morning. I'm going back to bed." I turned toward the door when he suddenly grabbed my shoulder and spun me back to face him, pushing me up against the wall. His forcefulness sent a shockwave up my spine. He had never touched me like that before. My insides froze. I took a breath trying to assess the bullying stranger standing in front of me. He was bigger than me by a foot of height and seventy-five pounds of weight. My heart raced as the fight-or-flight mechanism fired up, rummaging in my brain for an answer as he pinned me in place. My mind replayed the many phone calls I had had with his doctor over the past few months as David's behavior had gotten more erratic. He had been coaching me on how to respond to him if he became threatening.

"You have to protect yourself as well," he had told me when we spoke last. "I have known people in his deteriorating condition to do rash, unpredictable things." I could hardly believe I was having this conversation about someone who had been such a peace-loving, docile individual. The doctor suggested I use subterfuge if I ever felt in danger—and that was clearly now.

"Okay, I changed my mind," I said. "I'm hungry for breakfast too; let's go." As we drove, the doctor's advice continued to play in my head: "If he gets aggressive, take him to the hospital and let them take it from there." David was silent, looking out the window. I was still shaken from the shocking altercation, and I hoped I was doing the right thing. My nerves were a jangled mess and there was no one to call for help. Being deceptive with him felt wrong, but being physically pushed around did too. My body already felt depleted as the stress of the past few years had weakened my reserves. I understood now why David's mom had swerved off the road and crashed into a tree after falling asleep at the wheel; exhaustion had consumed her from caregiving for her husband. She escaped injury, but David's dad was airlifted to the emergency room and lived his remaining days in a nursing home. When we pulled up in front of the hospital, David noticed we were not at the restaurant. "What are we doing here?" he asked, clearly miffed.

"I just want to get your blood tested before we go eat," I lied again, trying to make it sound perfectly natural to get a blood test before a meal. But he wasn't having it and refused to get out of the car. Now what? Shuddering inside with fear and frustration, I entered the emergency room and asked for help bringing him in. The attendant came out with a wheelchair, but David refused to budge. When he told me they couldn't force him, I lost it. "What the hell am I supposed to do, then? I brought him here because I'm desperate for help," I cried out.

"I'm sorry, Sir. This is not only a hospital policy, but it's a state law that we can't force a grown man into the hospital unless he's a clear danger to himself or others," he explained. "He seems pretty quiet now." Oh, come on! What did he know?

"But he's a danger to me!" I exclaimed, "He knocked me up against the wall when I told him to go back to bed." I was waving a finger in David's direction, not caring whether he heard me or not.

"Did you call the police to report it?" he asked. Oh for god's sake—was he kidding me? This was going nowhere. The attendant turned and headed back to the hospital with the wheelchair, leaving me standing there in the parking lot. Exasperated, another idea popped into my head. I turned my attention back to David.

"Your mom asked me to make sure your blood sugar was okay, so I'm just doing what she asked." I held my breath and hoped that pulling out the 'beloved mom' card would work. Never mind that his mom had died, something I hoped he wouldn't remember. A puzzled look came over his face, and then he unbuckled his seat belt and got out of the car. I silently choked up with relief.

We walked through the entry doors and stood in line to register. As we waited, I fretted about whether this was going to backfire. If they don't find anything wrong, what will I do? If I take him back home, there's no telling what might happen. The painful fact was that I was scared of David. And I had no clue how to make any sense of that. The registrar motioned us to step forward.

"Who is the patient?" she asked.

"His name is David Jaeger," I pointed toward him. "I'm Steven Knipp, his partner and health guardian. I have his relevant information." She shoved a clipboard of forms in my hand. I had just started filling them out when I heard a loud thump on the floor as several people gasped. I spun around to find David flat on his back, not moving. Suddenly, the room was spinning with motion as healthcare workers descended on the scene. People were pointing and staring. David's eyes fluttered open as the staff checked his vital signs. A stretcher appeared and within seconds he was whisked into the back with me following close behind. After David was examined and no injuries were found, the doctor asked to speak to me in the hall. I was still rattled, trying to process what had just happened, the sound of his head thumping on the floor ricocheting in my ears.

"You said that David has Alzheimer's," she said. "Is he living at home with you?"

"Yes," I replied.

"How are things going?" My chest swelled up with pressure as the last year of accumulated stress came to a head.

"Not well," I said, followed by involuntary words that came spewing out. "He leaves the apartment in the middle of the night and I installed a door alarm that keeps me awake and I'm totally wiped out and I've tried everything and I don't think I can handle it and the reason I brought him here was my doctor suggested it," I stopped, catching my breath. The doctor listened carefully as I slowed down and told her about what had happened just preceding our visit.

"I understand; that's helpful to know," she said. "Do you feel capable of taking him home tonight?" She must have seen the panic spark in my eyes because before I could respond she added, "Listen, there's no medical reason to admit him but, given your circumstances, we could keep him overnight for observation if you wanted to get some rest." I burst into tears of relief. She put her hand on my shoulder. "Don't worry," she consoled me, her voice filled with compassion, "We can get this sorted out in the morning."

26

Breathe. 2012

was jolted awake by a loud ringing sound. Adrenaline rushed through my body and jet-fueled my thumping heart as I leapt out of bed. Was that the front door alarm? Had David left the apartment again? Wait. It's not that. Breathe. David wasn't here. He was safe. Breathe. The cobwebs in my brain began to clear. I picked up the telephone.

"Mr. Knipp, this is Dr. Martin," I heard the voice say. "David is fine; he's resting comfortably but he's asking for you. When might we see you today?" Everything flooded back. The altercation. The hospital parking lot and that useless attendant. David's collapse. The kind doctor. I took another deep breath and replied that I'd be there within the hour. Before we hung up, he added one more thing. "We won't be able to keep him for another night, so if you'd like, I can get our case manager to meet with you to talk through some options."

I was fully awake now. There was an utter stillness in the air as I slowly looked around the apartment. Being alone felt unnatural, but the thought of him coming back made my heart race. I couldn't do it anymore. Watching him night and day was going to break me, and now that he had become threatening, anything might happen.

My stomach began to unclench the knot it had been holding for months. The constant worry to keep a hypervigilant eye on David had littered my insides with tension. I had gotten so accustomed to being always 'on edge' that I hardly knew how to relax anymore. There would be time for that later. Right now, I needed to head to the hospital, which opened up a floodgate of unknowns. In what state would I find David? Would he be mad that I left him there last night? If he wasn't mad and just wants to go home, what do I say? Would he even remember what happened? The weight of it all threatened to put the knot right back in my stomach. Breathe. I threw on some clothes and headed to my car. As I drove the fifteen minutes to the hospital, my thoughts drifted back to a recent conversation with a coworker. Her dad was also struggling with Alzheimer's and she told me her Mom had enrolled him in a three-week program to assess his medications, which also gave her some time to recover from the exhaustion of caregiving. I had logged this information into the back of my brain and now seemed like a perfect time to mention this. By the time I was seated with the case manager, I had a plan. Cynthia, who I learned had a lot of experience with older folks, pulled out David's file.

"I've read over Mr. Jaeger's health history, and it looks like you need some assistance with his care. I was going to recommend an adult day center, but I can see you've already tried that. Did that not work out?"

I was ready for this. "Not well, no. He has not responded to either the day care setting or having people come to our house. But I do have an idea." I told her about the facility my coworker had described. Her eyes lit up.

"I know all about that program; it's a perfect interim plan. Having him assessed for his mental functioning will be helpful in placing him at the right facility to live out his life." My throat constricted and my eyes became watery. I hadn't gotten that far in my thinking. She was talking about a place he would live until he died; I was just trying to get some rest as he was evaluated—and yet what other option was there? Every part of me knew there was no going back. Cynthia concluded our meeting by telling me she could get everything arranged within the next few hours and would text me when the transportation vehicle had arrived to move David. I thanked her and then stepped back out into the hallway, trying to process the enormity of it all. My heart began to thump harder. Breathe. I took the long way to his room so I could take the time to formulate my words. How do I tell him how bad his mind had become and that I could no longer care for him? How was David going to react to all this? After fifteen minutes, I forced myself to step into his room.

"Are we going home?" he asked, the minute I opened the door. He was clearly ready, having already gotten dressed, and was now reaching for his shoes. There was a big grin on his face that stabbed me in the heart. I needed to state it fast or I was going to falter.

"I'll get you home as soon as possible, but I just met with the doctor and he thinks your medications are giving you some trouble." I paused to let it sink in. It was a partial fib, but easier to explain than the truth. I pressed on. "He suggested a place that specializes in monitoring your drugs and would like to transfer you there today. Is that okay?" David's eyebrows furrowed. He went back to his shoes, not replying. He stood after having them on and went for his coat. Had he heard me? I kept myself quiet until he was standing in front of me.

"When can we go?" he asked. I couldn't tell if he still meant home, or to the facility, so instead of asking him, I pretended he agreed to my request.

"They are sending over a transport ambulance soon. Let's go for a walk until they arrive." I held my breath that he'd go along with it and, with no hesitation, he followed me out of the hospital and into the courtyard. We found a bench and took a seat. The air was chilly and it was a clear fall day. I reached over and took his hand for reassurance, trying to be strong for both of us. The minutes seemed to stretch for hours. David wasn't speaking much, which wasn't unusual, but his silence dredged up my insecurities. Was I really doing the right thing? Should I take him home, quit work and try harder? In normal times, we would have worked this through together, so not having him to talk through this monu- mental decision left me with a crippling uncertainty. Finally, my phone buzzed with the social worker's text. Breathe. I stood up and forced my voice to sound chipper.

"Our ride is here." His face held an unexpressed question mark. "The doctor wants to make sure your pills are still working. They are taking you for more tests. You will be there for a few days." I held my breath. He nodded and mumbled 'okay,' then stood and followed me. I exhaled quietly. Taking his hand, we walked the short distance back to the hospital entrance where the ambulance transport vehicle was waiting. As we neared the atten- dant, I gave his hand a squeeze, "I'll be right behind you," I said, "and meet you there." I wanted to wrap my arms around him and tell him I loved him and missed him desperately and wanted so badly to have him back. I fought back the tears as he got into a wheelchair and was lifted onto the ambulance. As they strapped his wheelchair to the floor, I felt his gaze on me and we both smiled. He was still with me.

Tears pooled in my eyes as I trailed behind the transport vehicle. It was impossible to wrap my brain around his 180-degree shift in just 24 hours when he'd been so adamant and defiant. For the millionth time that day, I questioned whether to take him back home, but pushed it back down. I knew I was in over my head. There was no question we had both become endangered. Breathe.

Thirty minutes later, we had him settled into his room. It was simple, nothing fancy, but comfortable. It had the essentials—a twin bed, a nightstand, a dresser, and a television. There was a private bathroom that David had wandered into the minute he got there to relieve himself. A short while later, staff brought us dinner. We had missed the communal meal and most of the residents had already retired to their rooms. The facility was not large, housing only about thirty residents. As we ate, David kept looking around the space—perhaps to find something familiar—or a way out? I couldn't tell what he was thinking, but the expression on his face was placid, so I wasn't worried. It was breaking my heart to leave him here, but I reminded myself that he'd be safer, and I had to trust that the Universe had brought us here for good reason.

With dinner eaten and David settled into bed, I got up to leave. "I'll be back first thing in the morning," I said as he sat up and took my hand. "I love you and will see you tomorrow." He tightened his grip as if to say "stay" but let go once I began to walk towards the door. It took every bit of courage I could muster to leave his room.

I held it together until I was in the car and then felt my eyes start to well up. Driving home without him, his seat empty next to mine, sent a crushing wave of anguish through me. We had arrived at the point of no return, and I could barely handle what this turn of events meant for us. How many endings were left before he was gone forever? I pulled over to the side of the road to let the tears come.

Somehow, I managed to sleep through the night. My eyes were bloodshot and puffy from all my crying as I arrived back at the facility. The nurse met me at the entrance to give me an update from his first stay overnight. He had rested peacefully until getting up for breakfast. She pointed me to the area where David was sitting. My eyes swept the room, taking in the residents. Some were muttering to themselves; another was playing with her hair. When my eyes landed on David, I did a double take. He was simply staring out the window. When he noticed me, I saw a glimpse of recognition, but I could immediately tell that something had changed. Despite all the crying I had already done, seeing him like this still brought more tears. His body was slumped, giving the impression that he had given up, as though the disease had finally submerged him completely. He might as well have been 90 years old. I bit my lip to steady myself and moved in toward him.

"How are you this morning, dear?" I asked. He looked at me and shrugged, saying nothing. "Did you eat breakfast?" I scanned his face trying to gauge his current state of mind. He muttered something unintelligible, but I knew he meant that he had eaten.

The way we spoke now, which had been coming on slowly for months, was a kind of shorthand. His facial expressions and mumbles were like our very own Morse code. His capitulation was so complete that I couldn't help but blame myself. Was I wrong to take him to the hospital? Was it a mistake to have checked him into this place? Should I have just sucked it up and tried something else? As resolute as I was trying to be with my decision, the doubt was still eating away at me. We sat together as my mind reeled. After a few minutes, I kissed him on the head and made the short walk down the hall to the doctor's office. He stopped what he was doing, invited me to sit down, and got right to business. "We've taken him off the Alzheimer's drug he started when he was first diagnosed; he's beyond the stage when that remains effective. We will continue to monitor his blood sugar and other vital signs over the next few weeks." He went on to tell me more about their mental evaluation process, something I only partially listened to because I was still focused on what I saw in David.

"He seems to be completely resigned," I interjected, when there was a break in conversation. "Is this common?"

The doctor's words were blunt. "Yes, I've seen this many times. Patients with early-onset Alzheimer's, which can advance at a much faster pace, often seem to be confused or simply crash once they are moved from their familiar surroundings." The guilt closed in, nearly suffocating me. My mind flashed back to Hawaii. How could I have done this to him again? I should have known better. The doctor studied me for a minute as though he was trying to read my mind. "I was told what happened that prompted you to take him to the hospital and, as difficult as that must have been, you did the right thing." Our eyes met and the empathy in his expression choked me up. They were the words I needed so desperately to hear. I wasn't a bad person. I wasn't abandoning David.

I took a deep breath. "So what do we do next?"

"You should be prepared to transfer him to a 24/7 memory care facility once he's done here," he replied. The mention of this crushed me. There was truly no turning back now. Regardless, I needed to stay strong. We finished up our talk and I went to say goodbye to David, who was still in the same place I left him, sleeping. But when I reached over to touch his hand, he woke up and stared at me intently. Our eyes focused on each other, but neither of us spoke. I wondered if, in the depths of his incomprehension, there was an inkling of understanding that he was never coming home.

27

A Final Residence. 2013

The place we found for David was Gaffney House, a beautiful old home that had been modified into a memory care facility. It was a grand, stately building, built in the 1920s and filled with rich wood interiors. We had driven by the building hundreds of times over the years and wondered what it was. The social worker told us about it and, after she described the place, I felt super grateful that David's mom had left him enough money to pay for it. If David had to be anywhere, this was the place. The staff was highly skilled and, with only nine residents, they were each given exceptional care. I was encouraged to make David's bedroom feel like home, so I moved in some of our furnishings and family photographs. This was going to be his residence now, and while that was a hard truth to swallow, it made it easier to know that he was in good hands.

As soon as I got home that night, I lit up the fattest joint I could roll. I was so revved up that my mind needed a mood shift to calm down. Jetta followed me out to the back porch, hopping up onto my lap where I always sat to smoke and ponder. The events of the day shuffled through my mind. David's relocation from the treatment facility to Gaffney House was uneventful. Once he was inside and shown his bedroom, he was more interested in going back downstairs where the others were. Instead of stirring him up by saying goodbye and risking an upset, I slipped out the back door. This was suggested by the lead nurse as a way to acclimate David more easily to the other residents. And now I was at home, and he was living somewhere else, permanently. It felt wrong, upside-down somehow. Our twenty-plus years of cohabitation had ended. My mind swam in another direction as I exhaled. There was no way back to the way it was, and yet I was desperate to hold on. I wanted to remember David's sparkling hazel eyes that lit up my heart, filling me with hope. I wanted to remember that first time we were naked together, lying in his arms and feeling the safety of knowing he was going to be there for me. I wanted to remember his gentle, loving voice that assured me everything was going to be okay. When I got into bed that night, I grabbed his pillow and inhaled the scent of him, hoping to never forget.

I was still clinging to my memories of David when I arrived for my next visit. What I saw triggered internal alarm bells. I knew there would be an adjustment period, but his appearance was shocking. His face was unshaven, his clothes were stained with food, and the smell of a dirty diaper trailed behind him. The look on his face was pure annoyance. Even though I had seen pieces of this at home, I didn't expect to experience it here. When a staff member noticed my shock, he assured me they were watching him closely. "He's been a bit aggravated when we've offered to help him, so we're leaving him alone to see what he is capable of on his own so we can keep him as independent as possible." That made sense to me. I began to calm down. When I came back a few days later, he looked much better. I discovered that David had responded well to an attractive male attendant—no surprise there—and it didn't take long before he was back to his good-natured self. I was glad to see him all cleaned up and happy, especially since people were clamoring to see him.

Much like after his brain surgery, I had to set boundaries around visitors and manage their expectations. At first, David had quite a few people stop in who hadn't seen him in years. Most of them came to see him only once—they had a hard time dealing with the new David. He had a few church friends who made regular visits for a while, but it didn't take long before they, too, stopped coming. It worked out better anyway, because fewer visitors kept David more even keeled. We had, again, fallen into a comfortable routine. Nearly every day I would go to visit him, usually finding him on the couch, head drooped, asleep. I'd gently touch his leg and he'd open his eyes, smile, and ask, "Walk?" He would jibber-jabber as we walked around the block, a childlike babble of indistinct words that only I could follow. Arms linked together, walking slowly down the sidewalk, I'd tease him about his growing belly, or talk about Jetta or his mom and dad, the main things he still responded to. Even though his parents were both deceased, he didn't seem to remember. He would giggle and yammer on, making no sense but to me. We laughed together easily and often. It felt like we were both new people. I knew I had needed help with David, but I had no idea it would make such a huge difference. I had time to breathe again, to relax after work, to go out with friends for dinner, and to get back to the gym. It was like the old me was back and I could be there for him.

Slowly over time, David became more familiar with the other residents and definitely had his favorites. In particular was one woman who was always sitting by herself, endlessly repeating the phrase *come here, come here, come here, come here.* One day I arrived to find David in his chair next to her, smiling, listening to her repeat the mantra. I kept my distance and observed them. The woman was usually in a trance-like state, her eyes not wavering. Today she was glancing skittishly at David, her rhythm slowing, halting as he just sat there smiling at her. Then she stopped and looked directly at him. His face was aglow with loving kindness. She patted his hand, then slowly returned to her mantra but much more softly this time. There he was, I thought, his calming spirit fully intact. Even now, with his mental faculties considerably diminished, he was still a priest. The church had tried to take that away and failed, and now even Alzheimer's could not rob him of it.

That night as I sat in my regular spot with Jetta, it was impossible not to think about David as the spiritual healer he once was. It was an electrified presence I felt the minute I stepped into his office on that first day. And it wasn't just me; everyone felt it. I could still hear Oliver's words, a gay guy that was on the AIDS speaker's panel with me. "David saved my life," Oliver said to the audience. "He told me I didn't need to believe what I had heard in the church about gay people. That I had every right to seek the solace of my spiritual heritage. It was David's words and his reassurance that kept me from killing myself, which I nearly accomplished before meeting him." It didn't matter whether he was sitting quietly with someone as they dealt with sickness, or was speaking to hundreds during Mass, David's peaceful presence changed the hearts of people. It happened over and over again. And I got to be around that all the time.

This is why I fell so hard for him. He radiated an energy I couldn't resist. I was desperate to forget Tom's tragedy and my all-but-certain end. I wanted to love again before it was too late. We were the answer to each other's deepest fear: aloneness. How could I have possibly known what he would become for me, and I for him? He loved me unconditionally and promised to be there no matter what, and he was. And now it was my turn to repay his kindness.

As I continued ruminating about our remarkable life together, the resignation and defeat slammed into me. Together, we had fought our way through suicide, AIDS, cancer, mania, a brain tumor, and David's loss of his beloved priesthood. But there was no fighting Alzheimer's. There was no medication, no surgery. This had already defeated us. One day very soon, it would be over. Tears pooled in my eyes as this truth rained down on me. As if sensing my sadness, Jetta nuzzled me for another rub. As I petted her soft body, the theme from the AIDS retreat sprang to mind: "*Fearfully, wonderfully made.*" It was never clearer to me than now: life was both dreadfully fearful, and extraordinarily wonderful. David taught that to me.

28

The Silent Call. 2014

I was camping in the forest over the 4th of July weekend when an emergency call came from the facility. "David was just taken to the hospital," the attendant said, then quickly added, "He's going to be all right, but you should come as soon as you can. He keeps asking for you." She explained that, earlier in the day at the home, David had fallen down after vomiting a copious amount of food and fluid. He had been in assisted living for six months without incident, so the vomiting was alarming. Scrambling to get packed, and racing to the hospital, my mind was riddled with guilt and fear. Why did I decide to go camping? I lashed myself mentally for not being there. When I arrived at his room, I sighed with great relief. He wasn't comatose. He was sitting up and smiling.

"What happened to you?" I asked, trying to sound calmer than I felt. He was glad to see me, his whole face lighting up with a wide grin that acknowledged my presence. He replied with a few incoherent words, meaning he didn't know what happened. The doctor arrived a few minutes later.

"David was badly dehydrated, so that may have caused the fall," he explained, "but we're not sure about the vomiting. His blood sugar has been hard to control, so that could also be playing a role." The doctor asked to speak to me privately, so I followed him into the hallway. He got right to it. "You might want to consider hospice when he returns back to the home."

The word 'hospice' blew a hole in me. Were they suggesting it was over for him? "Isn't that for dying?" I exclaimed.

"I'm not saying he's dying right now," the doctor quickly replied, "but when he came in, he was confused and combative and we had to restrain him. It was very hard for him to go through that. If he's on hospice, the facility isn't legally required to send him to the hospital every time something like this happens." So much was coming at me all at once. Hospice. Restraint. I thought I was prepared for this, but how does anyone get ready? Nevertheless, I resigned myself to accepting this new reality.

David returned to the home a few days later and, over the next few weeks, I noticed more dramatic changes. He slept long hours during the day and roamed the halls at night. He wasn't able to walk around the block anymore, so we'd sit, mostly in silence. There was never a time that he didn't light up when I arrived. His eyes glowed with a recognition that was unmistakable. It was all we had left, really. I couldn't remember when he stopped using my name. Somewhere amid the trauma and chaos of the past year, my name had faded from his voice. It was so gradual that by the time it happened, I didn't think much about it. He would get my attention in other ways, like just vocalizing "Ste"..., or just "Ssss"..., and I knew he meant me. In the quietness of these visits, this loss was all the more glaring, though. Seeing that shimmer in his eye, the one that said "I know who you are" was what I lived for.

I was home with Jetta, curled up on the couch watching television, when a call came. It wasn't coming from the phone but, instead, from deep within me. David needed to see me, and an irresistible magnetic pull got me off the sofa, out the door, and into the car. On the way over, a recent conversation with Dr. Meredith played in my head. We had remained friends after she retired. We had been talking about end-of-life challenges for both the living and the dying.

"You want to give David permission to go, and let him know you'll be fine," she had said. There was so much to say that it was hard to know where to start.

I wanted to thank him for loving me and believing in me.

For lifting me up when I needed it most.

For his peaceful heart and depth of spirit.

And above all, for opening his heart and sharing everything about himself with me.

But how could I tell him goodbye? Had the time really come? The finality of it all engulfed me as I parked the car and walked up to the house. I took in a deep breath and trusted that whatever it was we needed to communicate would happen.

I found him sitting at the dining room table in a high-backed wheelchair, his head drooped in sleep. The room was empty and quiet, a haven of solitude for the mentally diminished. I pulled a chair next to his and sat up close, putting my hand on his leg. His eyes opened and that gleam appeared. He knew me. "Hi, dear," I said, putting my cheek next to his, "I love you." He smiled, looking at me with great interest. I kept going, "We've had such an amazing life together and I will never forget any of it." He continued looking closely, his eyes bright with understanding. A spark of recognition memory was beaming out of him and it shot me square in the chest. Suddenly I was whisked back to his office that very first time we met. He had the same expression of empathy and compassion then that was radiating from him now—a beautiful lucidity that had been missing for a long time. In a tearful whisper, I added, "I'm going to miss you when you're gone, but it's okay for you to go. I'll be all right." We sat there; our eyes frozen on each other.

My thoughts stalled in the wake of this spiritual moment, he and I connecting by pure feeling alone. We had an unspoken channel that didn't require me to verbalize everything that I wanted to communicate. He was there, with me, sensing what I felt. Without warning, a wave of gratitude soaked my entire being as forgiveness suddenly landed deep in my heart; in that instant we had both apologized for having to leave each other. I was immersed in a warmth of indescribable comfort. Then he leaned forward and whispered, "I gotta run now; I'm checking out." Wait. What? Did I hear that right? It was as clear as day and anyone who was there would have heard it. It floored me to think that, after over a year of incoherent mumbling, he was stating this monumental message with such clarity. There was no mistaking what he meant. That was why he had called out to me across the ether—to tell me it was time. With big tears of awe and gratitude, I smiled and whispered "Okay." As if noticing my emotional distress, he added, "But I'll be around." He smiled big, with a mischievous grin, and I lost it. I leaned my head on his shoulder and cried softly while he closed his eyes and went back to sleep.

29

Gone. 2014

The phone call came two days later. It was the nurse. "David's condition has changed. You should come as soon as possible." I'd been bracing for this since I last saw him, praying for it even. But now that it was here, I wanted to freeze time. With my heart in my throat, I got into the car and went to see him. Walking into his room, the first thing I heard was loud breathing. It was raspy. Rhythmic. Fast. He was lying on his back in bed on top of the covers, his head tilted back, mouth gaping open. And the breathing. The sound of it was primal, automated. Death was coming. I stood there, looking at him, but not wanting to touch him for fear of interrupting this sacred event. He had no awareness of me standing there; it was as though he was already lost into another world. I felt like a spectator to something I shouldn't be watching, as if it were a private experience, a holy one. He had told me just a few days earlier that he was checking out, and now that was exactly what my dear David was doing.

When I left his room and settled into the guest room next door, I felt numb. I crawled into bed and tried to put the images of him dying out of my head. Death was not a pretty process; it was disturbing to watch. As I stared at the ceiling, I remembered something he had told me not long after we met, that "if two people love each other, there can be no happy ending." How devastatingly true.

I was awakened by the sound of a knock on the door a few hours later. "I'm sorry, David is gone," the nurse said softly. As she turned and left, I took a deep breath to steel my nerves and walked across the hall to his room. The tomb-like silence struck me the minute I opened the door. He was gone. Whatever it was that animated his body had vanished as if it had never been there at all. His cheeks were sunken, his mouth open as if to say something. Forever silenced. My mind was emptied of thought as I placed my hand on his arm and looked at the remains of him. I had imagined this moment differently, that I would be wracked with grief and sobbing uncontrollably; instead I felt an overwhelming relief for both of us. I stood there, lost in time, his stillness permeating the space.

Suddenly, I had to get out of there. This body wasn't David. There was nothing of him here. I made it to my room and plopped on the bed as his last words rang through my mind, "I'll be around." As much as I wanted to believe what he had said, his words did little to relieve the aching emptiness in my heart.

30

The Eulogy. 2014

My body and mind were numb, my emotions shut down. I hadn't shed a tear since David's death and, instead of thinking too much about what that meant, I lost myself in the deluge of emails and phone calls from people wanting information about the funeral. David had chosen St. Ignatius as the location, a Jesuit parish that he and his mother had belonged to for several years. He knew his funeral would be controversial; people who felt he deserved to be kicked out of the priesthood might complain, so he was relieved when the priest said it would be okay. But now, with so many calls coming from people wanting to attend, I began to panic. St. Ignatius seated only 250 people and I feared it wouldn't be big enough. I placed a call to David's second-favorite parish, St. Joseph's. He had performed many Masses there over the years and, after coming out, he was one of the priests who said the Mass for Dignity, an organization for LGBTQ Catholics. I held my breath when I called to ask.

"That would be fine," the priest told me when I spoke to him on the phone. "We'd be honored to hold it here." It was perfect—a huge church that seated 750 people.

Planning a Catholic funeral was something we had done many times together, so I knew the drill: I needed a date, a church, a choir, a priest, a program, and food. David had already made a pact with his longtime friend Father Jeremy years ago; they had agreed that the other would perform the Mass for whomever died first. With that set, I posted the announcement and designed a website with all the specifics. I saved the most difficult part for last: preparing his eulogy. I had made the decision to deliver the only one, feeling strongly that it was time for people to know about us. They should know that David had not been alone through the public scandal and his subsequent ouster, that he had experienced love. I knew those that truly cared for him would want to hear that, and this was my last chance. The church made us hide our relationship for years, but we would have the final say.

As soon as people began to arrive at the parish on the day of his funeral, it was clear I had made the right call on the venue change. People were streaming in from everywhere. Retired priests, former parishioners, friends and family from all over the country. The church became jam packed, with the pews full and standing room only. There were easily 900 people. As I stood at the entry waiting for the procession to begin, I focused on the scent of incense and burning candles that filled the air. Light was streaming through the stained-glass windows, casting a warm glow through the soaring space and over everyone in attendance. This was like a second home to David and it made me feel closer to him. I returned my attention to those gathering around me as twenty-some priests poured in to jointly celebrate out of respect and admiration for David. I had met most of them over the years, but didn't know how much they knew about us being together. My heart began to pound as I realized what I was about to do—push our relationship right into their faces. There was no time to obsess about it though—the deep chords of the organ were suddenly ringing through the air, signaling the start of the procession. I took a deep breath to stay calm as people in the audience stood and turned their attention to the back of the church where we stood queued up. With all eyes on us, Father Jeremy began slowly to lead the way down the aisle. Holding David's framed picture above my head, I walked past the rows of people on either side. I glanced behind me as the casket was raised by six pall bearers and carried behind us, the solemnity of it catching in my throat. The long train of priests in full garb followed closely behind, the sound of their ritual garments swishing through the air. As we made our way toward the altar, I scanned the crowd and saw the faces of numerous people I recognized but hadn't seen for years. A lump formed in my throat as the full force of this day landed on me. David was gone and all these people were here to say goodbye. I was utterly overtaken with emotion by the multitude of lives David had touched. Hundreds of people had come to celebrate their beautiful, flawed priest. David must be blown away looking down at this incredible testament of acceptance and support. Then it struck me—was I going to ruin all this goodwill by spilling the beans about our relationship? Why was I doing this again? I felt the cold chill of blood running out of my face.

We arrived at the altar, my confidence shaken. What was I thinking? Was this whole thing more about me than us? I placed his photograph on a stand near the casket. And that's when I caught his smiling face. It was that same reassuring expression I had enjoyed so many times over our years together. That smile told me I could do this. We all took our seats and the music stopped, a hush falling over the cavernous space. Father Jeremy stepped out front and began to speak.

"Welcome, everyone," he began, "It's wonderful to see all of you gather to pay respects to this incredible priest that we were blessed to know." As he recited the ritual prayers of the funeral Mass for the next twenty minutes, uncertainty invaded my thoughts again. My heart started to thump as I imagined myself getting booed from the lectern, or worse. Doubt gripped me as the questions played over and over. Was I doing the right thing? Was this a huge mistake? As I watched Father Jeremy move about the altar, I remembered when David was standing up there and how courageous he had always been. He never wavered from saying that the church was wrong about gay people and how sex was something we all needed to get comfortable talking about. I sat through countless Masses listening to him challenge people to rethink their misguided perceptions. I took in the crowds of people to whom I was about to speak, almost everyone knowing what hell David had gone through with the church. The ones here today were his supporters. Of course they would understand. As the time for the eulogy approached, a beam of calm shone down on me. There was a palpable sense of David's presence beside me.

I took a deep breath and strode up to the lectern, catching a big smile from Gary, who sat near the front. He was the only person who knew what I was about to do, which gave me a jolt of confidence. When I had expressed my initial reservation about giving this kind of controversial eulogy, Gary replied without hesitation,

"To hell with everyone else. This is about you and David, period." And as if to underscore this assurance, Tom's voice penetrated my mind. *"I didn't give you the chance to say goodbye, but now you can. Do this for both David and me."* Before I lost it, I cleared my throat and moved toward the microphone.

"It is a privilege and an honor to be here with you today," I started, looking out at the sea of faces. "Most of you are familiar with David's ministry and public life, so I'd like to tell you something about his personal one instead. Having been his partner for the past 22 years has given me a unique perspective on him that I'd like to share." There, the secret was out; there was no turning back. A deafening silence rang in my ears, and I pushed ahead quickly before I lost my nerve. "When I met David, I had AIDS and there was no cure. Tom, my first partner, had just died of AIDS-related suicide. David loved me when most others wouldn't." With so many eyeballs on me, I caught glimpses of individual reactions. There were none that appeared incensed, and I focused on several heads nodding with understanding. For a moment, I was relieved, taking in the support from the audience. But then, two people suddenly got up and left. I sensed a few of the priests squirming in their seats on the altar. A swell of panic came over me, and it took every bit of self-control I could muster to keep from running out of the church. As I kept reading my prepared words, questions clamored in my mind. Can I really finish this? Should I? As if hearing my inner cries, David's words arose in my head: *Yes, you can and you should. Remember, we're doing this together.* A chill ran through me; he told me he'd be around, and he clearly was now. Emboldened by his words and bearing witness to the strength he had for all those years, I drove on to the finish.

"He knew he was taking a chance being with me, but he was prepared to give up the priesthood if our relationship ever became an issue. He lived what he believed was right: that relationship and intimacy are not at odds with being a priest; in fact, they made him better at it." As I spoke, I could feel my confidence urging me forward, my reservations gone. It was as if David were speaking through me. Twenty-two years of knowing this man and the gift of being loved by him rose up within me. Everything that he believed in, lived for, and suffered through was encapsulated in the words coming out of me now. "He often spoke of the delicate balancing act of being a priest with wanting intimacy and a relationship," I continued. "In theory, the two were not compatible, but David knew better." I paused for a moment and focused on a smiling face. The audience fell away as the closing sentences lined up in my mind.

"He was forced to choose between the church and love, and he wanted love more than anything. I will be forever grateful to him for that."

Epilogue

2024

Ten years after his death, I still feel David's presence within me. Everything I learned from him bubbles to the surface whenever he comes to mind. How to love unreservedly and without hesitation. To trust that the difficult moments in life can teach us something—and to embrace them just as we do the exhilarating ones. And his favorite quote about the three ingredients to happiness, "*Something to do, someone to love, and something to hope for,*" has become the measure by which I gauge whether my life is balanced.

While David was one of the greatest joys in my life, I am acutely aware that not everyone may feel empathetic toward him. One of the things that troubled me when I decided to author our story was how it might inflame deep feelings for those who have been victims of sexual abuse at the hands of priests, that their pain would be rekindled. But what I realized was that this issue must stay alive in the minds of the public if we want things to improve. Nothing will change if we don't keep talking about it. The damage that church policies and the resulting actions by some priests have caused in the lives of many believers is intolerable. Tossing out offending priests was nothing more than a stop-gap measure; the root of the problem will persist until the church acknowledges its culpability and abolishes mandatory celibacy. Sexual expression is a natural and necessary function of a healthy human being. Isn't that what people should expect in a servant of God?

David's tragic end knocked me down hard. He was such an amazing gift for so many years that his abrupt departure was impossible to process in any meaningful way. My grief was so overwhelming that all I could do was move on. I turned my focus to career and building new relationships. Two men had come into my life as David descended into the depths of Alzheimer's and offered the respite I desperately needed. Rusty and Jordan had been a couple when we met and the three of us quickly set up a new life together. It wasn't long, though, before my unprocessed grief began to bubble to the surface. After leaving my position at St. Vincent de Paul in 2018, I decided to start writing this memoir as a way to work through David's loss. In the meantime, I was hired as the Executive Director at GenPride, a non-profit organization focused on the lives of older LGBTQ people. Eventually, I was confronted with another issue I had not fully processed: the long-term impact of living with AIDS. My job had put me in contact with many older gay men who had also survived, and I began to see the effect of lives stripped of stable incomes, prior illnesses compromising current health, and social networks that were broken. Even while many in the mainstream assume that AIDS is over, it will never be for us. And while the drugs that initially saved our lives were a medical marvel, studies now report major health issues they can cause later in life. Essentially, feeling older than you are. That has certainly been my experience. Decades of life-saving medications coupled with the stress from a high-pressure job—exacerbated the cracks in my physical health. When I received a chronic kidney disease diagnosis in 2022, I made the tough choice to leave the workplace.

And yet, despite everything that has happened, reaching this season of life has been joyful. It has brought with it a willingness to *allow* the remaining moments to unfold. That alone has made moving through life easier. Even with rickety kidneys and achy joints, the fact that I've even reached retirement age at all is nothing short of miraculous; *I'm still here when I almost wasn't.*

Sometimes I sit and grapple with all the suffering that exists in the world. What is it all about? Everyone suffers, but what is the point? I know what David would say. He wrestled with these questions personally, and especially as he was burying men and women who had died of AIDS. I distinctly remember him saying in a talk he gave, quoting Pope John Paul II, that "the purpose of suffering is to release love into the world." He described it as a way to evoke compassion and kindness toward others, and to encourage necessary changes in our lives. That was true for us. It was my suffering that prompted me to reach out to David all those years ago, and it was his suffering that made him rethink how he wanted to experience love. It is when we suffer that we also realize how much we are connected and need each other. This was the case with the two men I loved and buried. We weathered our individual storms more easily because we were there for one another when things became unbearable. But while we stayed together through both the joys and the pains, we couldn't save each other from the inevitable: that every one of us comes to an end.

There is no living without the dying.

This inescapable truth ignites in us the mysterious reality of our existence: each of us is a distinctive, magnificent flame that burns brilliantly, albeit briefly, in the Universe.

Fearfully, wonderfully made, indeed.

Postscript

2003

Photo credit: Jan Starry, Prague.

David composed the following as a personal statement while he was on administrative leave from the priesthood. I've included it here to elicit memories for those who knew him.

Who I am.

I am David Jaeger, a lifelong Seattleite and a priest for 34 years. I did it backwards from most people. Very early I had discovered the spiritual world and made it the main theme of my life. Years later at age 45, I faced up to my sexuality and set about integrating the two sides of myself.

I arrived in the world on July 27, 1943; the first born and only son among the four children of my parents, Peter and Lorrayne.

I entered St. Benedict School in kindergarten. I discovered the first time I entered our parish church that I wanted my life to be about communing with God in company of other people through the Church. I did well in school and I grew up with good friends. At the same time, I felt different from my peers—both in my desire to be a priest, and in strangely being almost the only one who saw no difficulty with what was required to be a priest: neither to date nor ever get married.

I convinced my parents (over their protest) to let me enter the seminary at age 15. I spent the next 11 years finishing high school, college and theology studies at St. Edward and St. Thomas Seminaries—to arrive at what had to be the happiest day of my life when I became a priest.

I served as a young priest in two parishes for six years total, three years as director of the Archdiocese's youth programs, then for eleven years with men interested in studying for the priesthood, while also doing parish work—preaching, teaching, counseling, Masses, funerals and weddings.

Being homosexual (without saying so even to myself) and celibate, I learned next to nothing in all this time about my sexuality and was inexperienced—even though I began to be curious about it after I finished seminary at age 26. But I matured very slowly and inadequately in this area of life until I was 45.

I had loved practically every minute of being a priest—especially all the people contact I enjoyed through ministry; and I also became involved in the peace movement. But at age 45, after an accusation of sexual misconduct, I finally entered into therapy and began to deal with my undeveloped sexuality and intimacy experiences. I grew relatively fast, and managed not to act too adolescent even though that was what I was in these areas. A combination of the growth I had already achieved in other areas of my life, therapists I worked with, and some newly found friends helped me to catch up. My life—spiritual, emotional and relational—expanded enormously and I discovered that I became more effective in my family and personal relationships as well as in my ministry, in addition to discovering great, new levels of happiness.

During this time I had the opportunity to specialize in working with persons with HIV/AIDS and gay and lesbian Catholics, with their families, with caregivers; and I advocated for the understanding of them and their lives among my fellow ministers in the Church, and the people I served in parishes. It was a great arena in which I learned more about myself through associating with people who had already developed more normally in the ways I had kept closed off to myself. At the same time I brought to bear in my new specialized work what I had learned thus far in my life in the worlds of religion and spirituality.

The Relationship Between Spirituality and Religion

The Spiritual:

Spirit (a metaphorical word meaning "breath") suggests that which is unseen, ungraspable, beyond control, yet vital, critical, inhering in and through all that lives and exists.

Every generation gives witness to its sense of the spiritual through stories, symbols, rituals, art, and music. Traditions (the word suggests what is "handed on" from person to persons and generation to generation) pervade all known history, in every era and culture.

At the spiritual level, people seek their meaning, their purpose, their call, their connection with others and the universe, their destiny, their healing, their relationship with what is prior to and beyond this life.

Through their spiritual connection people contribute to their relationships and don't demand more than a relationship can give.

They gain access to the spiritual through pondering the depths of their own experience, through traditions and practices and through sharing with others.

Religions

As a pathway: Religions perform the vital function—through creating and passing on language, story and symbol—of sharing people's spiritual experiences of old and the traditions through which they are accessed.

As an obstacle: Religions are also organized and develop in the midst of unfolding human history and culture and politics. As such they are regularly co-opted by powers and purposes that are not particularly spiritual, and can be used to enforce values and codes of conduct that are considered critical to the particular political configurations of limited times and places. In this way individuals and segments of society have often been excluded from the religious world—to the spiritual and social detriment of both the excluded and included.

The excluded: Homosexual and gender-variant people are only a couple of the groups that have been deprived of their rightful spiritual heritage. There are also divorced persons, persons in second marriages, prisoners, the poor, etc. Significantly, these people are not at the same time deprived of spiritual experience. Sometimes these people's spiritual experience is even deeper and purer for their distance from religious forms, because religious forms can sometimes be made ends in themselves rather than pathways to personal and shared spiritual experience and development. It turns out those inside and outside religious circles have much to offer each other.

The best of both worlds: It is possible, despite what many say, to be true to one's own person and spiritual experience and still benefit from what religions have to offer.

The present moment spiritually: In a world that is mysterious and beautiful, but one that is also filled with new challenges and fraught dangers, I continue today, formally on leave from active ministry as a priest, to journey with many people as a teacher, counselor and friend.

What I Believe.

How lovely on the mountains are the feet of one
Who brings good news!
Announcing peace, proclaiming news of happiness...

From my earliest years I desired with all my heart to have, as in the lines of this song I love, the feet of one who brings good news. At age 5, I pictured myself already as the priest I became 21 years later. Even though I experienced my limitations and the sharp edges of the church all through my life, my most profound and abiding experience in life and church was always the good news of God's love—bad or harsh notes never drowned out the beautiful music.

My Christian formation taught me that God became flesh and blood and lived a life like ours. I also experienced God in other religious traditions and cultures. I heard the call to respect and seek solidarity with every other person God made, and to seek peace with the planet and with all nations and peoples. Above all and throughout all, I came to realize that our first and continuous task is to become aware of and hold fast to the infinite, flesh and blood, love, care and appreciation that God has for us personally, and from there to embody that love in our relationships with others.

All these things came to me in the very earthy church world I lived in—through music, in sacred spaces, in colors and fabrics, in stained glass windows, statues and paintings, in words both sacred and informal, in rituals using water, bread, wine, oil, candles, and incense. Most effectively they came to me through people: parents and family, dear friends, relatives, and fellow believers; through sisters, priests and bishops, through preachers, ministers and members of many other Traditions, through non-believers as well.

The second verse of the song, *Out from the tomb, he came with grace and majesty; He is alive!* takes the longest to learn: that life and growth come also through a process of dying, of loss, involving insecurity and pain. Dying the way Jesus did—with awesome forgiveness and trust, the glory breaking through even as he was going through what the human race does to God among us—is the most awesome thing Jesus did. *Out from the tomb—with grace and majesty.* It is our calling: to be reborn over and over, and to rise from our deaths to deeper and more vibrant living. To have hope that in the midst of everything, our most important work is to experience that God (or whatever we may call that mysterious being) is on our side, endlessly loving and understanding us, helping us realize that apparent losses and threats are really stages toward transformation to a better self and a better world.

David Jaeger, 2003.

Acknowledgements

It didn't take long before I realized that while my job was to compose every sentence, writing and publishing a book is by no means a solitary process. I asked Ingrid Ricks, a writer and developmental editor whom I met in a writing class, to read my first draft. She reacted encouragingly to the story, and then promptly recommended I start over to make it the best it could be. It was excellent advice. She offered to coach me through structuring the story, and this began a multi-year working relationship. Ingrid also encouraged me to keep going when I felt overwhelmed emotionally, reminding me that our story needed to be told and that I was the only one who could tell it. She taught me a lot about how to craft a story, but it was her laser-focused and inquisitive mind that helped me most to bring our story to life.

Special thanks to my early readers: Irene Calvo, Nate Stokes, Molly McAllister, Meaghan O'Leary, Kathleen Jorgenson, Jessica Litwak, Gary Cole, and Kevin O'Brien. They read my drafts and gave me feedback that I was able to use to strengthen our story. I am grateful for their generosity.

* * *

Please leave a review at your favorite book site.
Thank you!

ISBN: 979-8-9915715-0-0

Developmental Editor: Ingrid Ricks, www.ingridricks.com

Copy Editor: Irene Calvo, www.CalvoEditing.com

Cover Art by: Sam Sohisoli

Interior Title Art: Sophia Litwak

Contact the author: stevenknippmemoir@gmail.com

www.ingramcontent.com/pod-product-compliance
Lightning Source LLC
Chambersburg PA
CBHW020227130626
46549CB00005B/1782